Third Generation Leadership and the Locus of Control

For my grandchildren's grandchildren:
may the world you inherit be free from the narrow-band thinking
and fear-driven behaviour that we so frequently encounter today.

Third Generation Leadership and the Locus of Control

Knowledge, Change and Neuroscience

DOUGLAS G. LONG

Routledge
Taylor & Francis Group

LONDON AND NEW YORK

First published 2012 by Gower Publishing

Published 2016 by Routledge
2 Park Square, Milton Park, Abingdon, Oxon OX14 4RN
711 Third Avenue, New York, NY 10017, USA

First issued in paperback 2017

Routledge is an imprint of the Taylor & Francis Group, an informa business

Gower Applied Business Research
Our programme provides leaders, practitioners, scholars and researchers with thought provoking, cutting edge books that combine conceptual insights, interdisciplinary rigour and practical relevance in key areas of business and management.

British Library Cataloguing in Publication Data
Long, Douglas G.
  Third generation leadership and the locus of control :
  knowledge, change and neuroscience.
  1. Leadership. 2. Leadership--Psychological aspects.
  3. Limbic system.
  I. Title
  158.4-dc23

Library of Congress Cataloging-in-Publication Data
Long, Douglas G.
  Third generation leadership and the locus of control : knowledge, change, and neuroscience / by Douglas G. Long.
      p. cm.
  Includes bibliographical references and index.
  ISBN 978-1-4094-4453-4 (hbk) -- ISBN 978-1-4094-4454-1 (ebk)
  1. Leadership. 2. Leadership--Psychological aspects. 3. Limbic system. I. Title.
  HD57.7.L6646 2012
  658.4'092--dc23

                                                                      2012006175

ISBN 13: 978-1-138-11579-8 (pbk)
ISBN 13: 978-1-4094-4453-4 (hbk)

Contents

PART THREE   CREATE THE FUTURE

List of Figures and Tables

Figures

Tables

About the Author

Douglas G. Long was born in New Zealand but moved to Australia in 1976. His tertiary education was in New Zealand, Australia, England and the United States, culminating in 1985 with a PhD in Organisational Psychology.

For many years he taught in universities in Australia and the United States including David Syme Business School, RMIT Graduate College of Management and Drexel University. From 1988 to 2000 he was associated with Macquarie Graduate School of Management in Sydney where he researched, designed and delivered the programme Leadership in Senior Management. Since 2003 he has held a post as a Casual Academic with Australia's Southern Cross University Graduate College of Management where he supervises candidates studying for their degree of DBA.

Along with this, he has been an active consultant specialising in leadership and change with public and private sector clients throughout Australia, New Zealand and South East Asia. In this role he has facilitated some major changes undergone by very large Australian and South East Asian organisations. He is an accomplished public speaker and public speaking has taken him to conferences in Australia, New Zealand, Singapore, Malaysia, Japan, The Netherlands, Finland, Spain, Brazil and the United States.

He has been involved in community service for most of his life. For 16 years he was a member of the St John Ambulance Brigade and, in Melbourne, after he was appointed a Justice of the Peace, he sat on the Bench at two local Magistrates' Courts for several years. In 1983 he was brought in to coordinate the State Relief Centre operations for the disastrous Ash Wednesday Bush Fires in Victoria.

Douglas now lives in Sydney, Australia, and is married with five children and four grandchildren.

He is the author of four earlier books:

- *Learner Managed Learning: The Key to Lifelong Learning and Development*

- *Competitive Advantage in the 21st Century: From Vision into Action*

- *The Challenge of the Diamond*

- *Leaders: Diamonds or Cubic Zirconia? Asia Pacific Leaders on Leadership*

And a co-author (with Andrew Mowat and John Corrigan) of:

- *The Success Zone: 5 Powerful Steps for Growing Yourself and Leading Others*

Prologue

On 25 May 1878 the Gilbert and Sullivan light opera *H.M.S. Pinafore* opened in London. In this work Ralph Rackstraw, a 'common sailor', and Josephine Corcoran, the daughter of his ship's captain, fall in love – a love that is doomed because of the difference in their social stations. However, Little Buttercup, a woman selling goods to the ships complement, makes the startling admission that, many years before when she was a nursemaid, she mixed up two children. Little Buttercup makes amends for her error by making it clear that Ralph Rackstraw is, in reality, the patrician who should be captain and vice versa. She says she cared for two children, Ralph Rackstraw and the captain, but that she returned them to the wrong parents. Once this is known, the two switch places and love blossoms.

Gilbert's lyrics were, in part, drawing attention to the sometimes farcical situation in which command – leadership – belonged to people by right of birth and had nothing whatsoever to do with experience, competence or training.

Of course, even back then, there were some areas in which this approach had to be modified. In the commercial world a person's status determined whether or not they could be considered for management but, once a person having appropriate social standing had entered an organisation, there was no doubt that promotions would come based on length of service while those lacking appropriate social status would not be promoted. Seniority in terms of social status plus length of service determined one's place in the leadership hierarchy.

This was the world of First Generation Leadership and 1G Leaders (or Leadership 1.0). A person's birth determined their place in society and, therefore, their ability to lead. In the 1950s and 1960s this was still a significant (even if diminishing) factor.

Today, at least in developed countries, this style of leadership is less encountered and even less accepted. We live in a world that has moved on to 2G Leadership, based on conformance and compliance, but in which a new approach – Third Generation Leadership and 3G Leaders – is increasingly demanded across the board.

This book explores the evolution to Third Generation Leadership and then provides information as to how, through knowledge and application of learning derived from neuroscience, each of us can become 3G Leaders.

Third Generation Leadership is the component that can draw together the various leadership approaches being used by any organisation so that the leadership provided in the twenty-first century is increasingly effective.

Successful organisations in the twenty-first century will be those in which Third Generation Leadership is the norm.

Introduction

The defining moments of the first few years of the twenty-first century are probably the events of 11 September 2001 and the death of Osama Bin Laden on 2 May 2011. Like many other people, at least in the Western world, I was appalled at the events of 9/11 but shed no tears at the demise of Bin Laden.

There is a sense in which these events have significance other than their association with terrorism, however, and that is their symbolism in relation to the sort of leadership that has been extant for many years – a leadership approach in which power and force is used to enforce ideas and activities on others.

Over many years I have felt frustration created by my observations of the ongoing turmoil around the world and the apparent inability or unwillingness of many in academia, the media, politics, business, religious organisations and society at large to seriously question the underlying issues. My awareness of the inability of current leadership approaches to deal effectively with the ensuing mess has built up over a long time. But the trigger for the writing of this book occurred only in the recent past.

In the name of 'leadership', over recent years, we have seen increasing amounts of discriminatory, certainly immoral and possibly illegal behaviour by leaders in the political, business, religious and social arenas. As a result of such 'leadership', during the first decade of the twenty-first century, we have seen enormous increases in matters such as terrorism, wars of choice, development of empires, and a huge widening of the gulf between the 'haves' and the 'have nots' – especially in the Western world.

I have been prompted to act because of these most recent observations of what was happening both in Australia and internationally.

I was a child in the 1940s and 1950s. During this time I learned of how, not too long before, part of my mother's family had fled to England from a totalitarian regime in the Baltic region. Her family went as refugees first to England and then to the Antipodes. Here, like so many other refugees and/or migrants, they had rebuilt their lives.

I learned of the totalitarian regime that had later existed in Germany and how the Nazis gradually subverted the law until they could persecute whoever they wished in their quest for world dominance – the result was concentration camps, gas chambers and mass murders as well as the whole disaster of the Second World War.

As I grew up I became increasingly aware of the abuses occurring in the then USSR. I learned of people being imprisoned without trial on the unsubstantiated complaint of a few informers; I read of the gulags in Siberia; I heard about the Secret Police and their right to interrogate without the suspect having any form of legal representation or any legal redress – or even knowing what evidence they needed to refute. I learned how the decision of one or two people who had power could destroy the lives of many because of an absence of any form of democracy. I was led to believe that at least the United States, Great Britain, Canada, Australia and New Zealand were bastions of freedom where such abuses could never occur and in which no religious faith would ever be singled out or denigrated. I learned I could trust those who led my country and the 'free world' because, even though they sometimes made mistakes, they were people of integrity and high moral standing.

I was brought up in a Christian tradition which taught me that the underpinning of my faith was unconditional love and respect for all people. For many years I was active in the evangelical traditions of the Baptist and Anglican Churches in New Zealand and Australia. I learned that what was preached was one thing: too often, what was done was something else. Like many others, I learned to compartmentalise my life and how to apply 'conditional respect' for others.

I became a soldier and during my service New Zealand became involved in a war – Vietnam – on the premise that by stopping the communists there we would maintain our freedoms and we would ensure that no subversion of our laws, rights and freedoms would ever occur. When I was commissioned I, along with all fellow officers, was reminded that part of my role was to preserve those laws and the freedoms that we then enjoyed.

Eventually I realised that a compartmentalised life was ultimately destructive and I decided to try to actually enact what I espoused. I realised that the only base for a fair and free society was unconditional respect for all people regardless of age, colour, race, religious faith, sexual orientation, or any other discriminating factor. I learned that true leadership requires this as a core foundation element.

I moved to Australia and a few years later I was appointed a Justice of the Peace in the State of Victoria. In those days in Victoria some Justices of the Peace also functioned as Honorary Justices (also known as Honorary Magistrates) and were empowered to administer justice in the Court system. I became one of these. During the swearing-in ceremony as an Honorary Justice at the Supreme Court in Melbourne the Chief Justice of Victoria reminded those of us being sworn in that, as persons now empowered to fix bail for accused persons, to sentence guilty people to periods of imprisonment and/or to impose monetary penalties, to authorise search warrants, to issue arrest warrants, and perform other activities involved in the legal process we had to ensure that we did not abuse our powers nor allow others to abuse the legal system – the rights of all people were to be respected in the administration of justice.

I am now in my sixties and I weep for what is happening in Australia (and, indeed, around 'the free world') in politics, religion and social justice.

I have spent my life believing in the power of a democratic society where the rule of law ensures that people will not be imprisoned without trial; that habeas corpus is a vital component of a free society; that secret police and interrogation without legal representation is wrong and an abuse of power; that freedom of faith, speech and association are inalienable rights – even if I disagree totally with what you say, believe or with whom you associate, you have an absolute right to say what you want, follow the faith or non-faith of your choice, and associate with whoever you wish. But it is clear that much of what I once believed and experienced as being normal no longer pertains.

The United States, Great Britain and Australia are no longer the bastions of freedom where leaders are people of integrity and undoubted high moral standards – I am unsure about Canada and New Zealand.

I have seen our leaders lie, obfuscate, twist and turn in order to avoid accountability while furthering agendas that have nothing to do with freedom but everything to do with power and pandering to special interest groups. I find that it is now possible in the United States to imprison without trial even American citizens and to deny them any form of justice. I find that the United States can set up its own gulags and concentration camps in which torture and abuse of legal process are acknowledged to exist. I find my own government compliant in this and, accordingly, guilty by association. I find that in Australia it is possible for secret police to determine that a person is a security risk and, without disclosing to him or any other party the evidence or information they have collected, imprison and deport him even though he was here on a legal visa. I find my government wanting to pass laws that are capable of even further removing my civil rights of free speech, free movement and free association.

And I am reminded of what happened in Germany with the rise of Nazism and what happened in the USSR during the communist regime.

For where are the people speaking out against this move toward a possible totalitarian state? Many people who are worried about what is happening are compliant out of fear that they will be labelled terrorist-sympathisers or something similar; the Churches seem to have been seduced into thinking that Christianity has nothing to do with peace, freedom and human rights – the evidence of the Bible notwithstanding; our major established media are dominated by moguls who are too close to the government and, as was evident over the invasions of Iraq and Afghanistan as well as over the issues in other places like Iran, prepared to be mouthpieces for government propaganda rather than 'the fourth estate' which will challenge and hold governments to account. And when there are breaches of this 'cone of silence' such as has occurred with WikiLeaks, the emphasis is on finding and punishing those who dared to get the truth to the world rather than on correcting the wrongs disclosed.

Many years ago, Pastor Martin Niemöller in Germany wrote a well known piece lamenting indifference to abuses and atrocities conducted in Nazi Germany. He spoke of general indifference and inaction regarding Nazi treatment of the Jews, communists and trade unionists before concluding:

> *Then they came for me and there was no one left to speak out for me.*

Unless we see some real leadership that challenges current political, business and social agendas, then I foresee that Niemöller's words from yesterday may well be our epitaph tomorrow. Our existing approaches to leadership are clearly not working – and we live in the mess that is evidence of the failure of existing leadership approaches.

For years I sought to understand the leadership and followership that not only allowed, but at least tacitly supported, situations such as, at an earlier time, apartheid in South Africa, China's annexation of Tibet and their treatment of ethnic minorities, and more recently the invasions of Iraq and Afghanistan, the ongoing fiasco in the Middle East, the continual turmoil in so many parts of Africa, conflicts within what was once the USSR, and also, but a little later, the excesses that led to the global financial crisis of 2008, and, of course, the ongoing issue relating to the treatment of refugees and asylum seekers. From this I have sought to explore a leadership concept that might provide a path forward so that the world we bequeath to our children, grandchildren, and our grandchildren's grandchildren might be a far better one than that which exists today.

I call this world, the world of Third Generation Leadership – of course it could and can equally be called 3G Leaders or Leadership 3.0.

On this journey I have been helped by many people. Perhaps I should nominate all of them but two key influences have been John Corrigan and Andrew Mowat of Group 8 Education. Their research and learning in the education sector, coupled with their openness and willingness to share, has been probably the most significant factor in helping me understand and explore this new world.

I also wish to acknowledge the support given by Tony Scotland, Lewis Kaplan, Colin Rymer, Ian Freeman, Cal Downs, Warren Blight, Gail Jeltes, Gail Hickey, Michelle Thompson and Renee Zacher (together with John Corrigan and Andrew Mowat) in reading through early drafts of the book and making suggestions that have been of considerable assistance in fine-tuning the work.

Just one note about the examples used to illustrate my arguments in this book. Every example is factual but in most cases some minor details have been changed in order to protect the identity of individuals and organisations. Where the example is a matter of public record, or where permission has been obtained, no such modification has occurred.

So far as I am aware, all sources have been attributed. However, in researching for this book I covered a very wide range of material from a broad variety of sources. If I have inadvertently reproduced material without appropriate acknowledgement I apologise unreservedly.

PART ONE
Understand the Past

In which we consider the leadership approaches that dominate today

1

The Background to Third Generation Leadership

Once upon a time, way back in the days when the earth was thought to be flat and dinosaurs roamed, back in the times before my father was a little boy, there were two types of people: first there were the rich and the powerful; and then there was everyone else.

In this world, the rich and powerful owned property and businesses. They provided jobs and produced the goods and services that everyone needed. Many of these people had taken risks in setting up their businesses – they had invested their money to create a business and they wanted to make a lot more money as a result. To do this they employed only the minimum number of people and they kept the wages low. Very often they made their employees work long hours in poor conditions. They rented out their properties at the highest possible figure and they sold their goods and services at the highest possible price. The result was that the rich became even more rich and, well, after all, what did the rest matter? Naturally, everyone wanted to be rich! But, as the old song puts it:[1]

> There's nothing surer; the rich get rich and the poor get poorer.

Of course, those people who weren't rich didn't like this situation at all. But nobody listened to them. The rich made the rules and, no matter what might be said, in reality the rules were designed to help them become even more rich and powerful.

In around 1899 Henry Ralph Harvey Chalmers joined the Bank of New Zealand (BNZ) as a junior clerk.[2] In 1957 he finished his association with BNZ

---

1   'Ain't We Got Fun?', 1921, lyrics by Raymond B. Egan and Gus Kahn.
2   The story of the Bank of New Zealand, in which H.R.H. Chalmers receives mention, is told in N.M. Chappell, *New Zealand Banker's Hundred: Bank of New Zealand 1861–1961*, 1961, Bank of New Zealand, Wellington.

as chairman. Over the intervening 58 years he had moved steadily through the ranks until becoming general manager, and then, after retirement, first a director and ultimately chairman. The only time he was not employed by BNZ was during the First World War when, as a soldier, he fought on the Somme. Harry, as he was known, was certainly intelligent but he received no formal academic, skills or management training over his entire working life. His was a fairly typical success story for the first half of the twentieth century: join a big organisation, work hard, do as you are told, ensure you don't seriously blot your copy book, and take every promotion offered no matter what the inconvenience. Harry, my paternal grandmother's brother, died in 1971 and I was present at the funeral where he was rightly hailed as one who had made a significant contribution to both banking and to society at large in New Zealand.

My Uncle Harry was a typical 1G Leader (First Generation Leadership is based on compliance – see Chapter 3) – a manager in a First Generation Leadership organisation – who operated very effectively both at work and in the family primarily in a somewhat paternal, command and control format.

My secondary schooling was at Auckland Grammar School, a boys-only state school in New Zealand. Auckland Grammar, like most other schools of the era in those long-gone days, had a proud history of caning miscreants. (I must stress that Auckland Grammar changed this approach many years ago.) In my day, one Master started his first class with new students by giving a lecture on the physics relating to the most effective way of caning (i.e. causing the most pain) complete with stick diagrams drawn on the board to illustrate his points. Another Master would chalk a 'magic circle' at the top of a flight of stairs and, after you had stepped into the circle and bent over, he would cane you – the contest was to ensure you didn't fall face-first down the stairs on impact. Yet another Master once stated he would cane (three strokes each) every boy in our class of 35 if anyone again interrupted his lecture. We made sure he had to cane us all during that class and I understand he never again made a similar threat!

In around 1958 Terry McLisky joined Auckland Grammar School as a maths and physics teacher. I was fortunate to have him as my teacher in both subjects for two years. Terry was different. I remember in his first class with us he suggested that if we wanted to learn we should sit at the front: if not, sit at the back and 'do what you like but don't interrupt the class'. I can recall only a few instances when any student sat at the back and I have no recollection of Terry ever resorting to the cane or even detentions in order to maintain attention.

Terry McLisky was a typical 2G Leader (Second Generation Leadership is based on conformance – see Chapter 4) – one of several at Auckland Grammar and other schools who were somewhat ahead of their time – who saw that encouraging conformance through the provision of positive reinforcement, such as personalised teaching and showing students that he really wanted to help them, would get far better results than enforcing obedience.

Today the world has moved beyond both Harry Chalmers and Terry McLisky. Since the 1980s the rapid development of computer technology, the Internet and social networking has revolutionised our access to knowledge as well as the way in which we interact. Those of us who completed our schooling in the 1950s and 1960s may have some difficulty in this new world, but those who have been schooled since the 1980s can hardly even imagine anything else. To understand this shift we need to understand the underpinnings of leadership.

Over the years emphasis has been placed on leadership traits, leadership attitudes and leadership behaviours. Much research has been done into each of these and myriad books have been written explaining why one or the other (or what combination of the three) is necessary for effective leadership.[3] For some 50 years there have been leadership training programmes of varying degrees of effectiveness and quality and there are champions and success stories for every approach that has been developed. We needed the work done by this research and these programmes.

Traditional approaches to leadership have not paid much attention to the world of neuroscience – mainly because the research that enables us to have these new understandings was not possible until relatively recently. Accordingly, as I say, we have been given models of leadership that are based on physical or character traits, attitudes and/or behaviours. We have been told that the activities of a leader are contingent on the situation in which the leader finds him or herself; we have learned that we can develop new attitudes; and we have been told to develop appropriate habits in order to provide effective leadership. Almost all of the approaches that have been developed are underpinned by serious, peer-reviewed research and they stand up to scrutiny. They have been used effectively by individuals and organisations across the globe with, understandably, differing cultures finding some leadership approaches more appropriate than others. They have made

---

3   See the Additional Resources section in the Appendix for a partial list of leadership material currently available.

a powerful contribution to the way in which we lead people today, whether in government, the military, business, school, society at large, or in the home.

But now they have either reached, or are very close to reaching, their 'use by date'. Unfortunately it seems that much of the currently available leadership material fails to realise this. This lack of awareness relating to 'use by date' is then reflected in the leadership education and training provided in many institutions and organisations.

When, from 1988 to 2001, I was conducting the programme *Leadership in Senior Management* at Macquarie Graduate School of Management in Sydney, a regular comment from participants was that the programme was different from what they expected. Consistently (but fortunately only from a minority of participants) came the comment that they expected to concentrate on how the leader interacted with his or her followers. These participants were seeking information on how to deal with the different situations in which leadership was exercised or assistance on how to deal with the interpersonal relationships of leadership interactions. Instead, what the 90 or so participants each year got was a programme that looked at leadership from a macro perspective – leadership as it impacted on total organisational performance through drawing together the variables that ultimately determine success or failure – and dealing with different situations and/or with interpersonal relationships is only a small part of this. *Leadership in Senior Management* was significantly different from most other leadership programmes being offered in Australia and was not popular with some of my academic friends because it was based on a different research base and promoted a different leadership perspective from that with which they were most comfortable.

Back in the early 1950s I remember being introduced to Gershwin's *Porgy and Bess*.[4] In that show there is a song, 'It Ain't Necessarily So', which points out that even if something is written in the Bible it may not be entirely accurate.

My parents strongly disapproved of this song and, therefore, of *Porgy and Bess*. They were devout evangelical Baptists and the thought of questioning what the Bible said was totally unacceptable – they were appalled when one day I came home from a friend's house and I was singing the lyrics. Perhaps that was why, as a developing youth, I continued to sing them when I was

---

4   Ira and George Gershwin, 1935.

frustrated about getting my own way! Perhaps, too, it was one of the reasons why, many years later, among other things, I studied theology!

But these words used to come back to me whenever people questioned why I taught a different approach to leadership from that which was in the majority of texts, articles and popular books. I needed to point out that just because traditionally the 'authorities' have told us that 'leadership' is this or that, doesn't necessarily mean they are right. Close examination of the fine print and a careful observation of reality just might alert us to the fact that 'it ain't necessarily so'!

Today the developing study of modern neuroscience has enabled us to look at a whole raft of things a little differently. Included on this raft is the matter of leadership.

One key issue that has arisen from the field of neuroscience relates to the brain's locus of control. The role of this book is neither to give a comprehensive overview of modern neuroscience nor to argue the pros and cons of the various theories that have emerged. Rather, this book utilises learning from only a very small aspect of modern neuroscience. In this book I utilise a basic understanding of the areas of the brain that control our attitudes and behaviours as these relate to the leadership function.

Jonah Lehrer[5] is one of the writers on neuroscience who has provided a simple way of understanding how the brain has developed and the manner in which our emotions impact on every part. Between 2002 and 2006 I was involved with research in state and Catholic schools in Victoria, Australia and in England. (The research was lead by John Corrigan.) Data was obtained from some 50 schools (almost all secondary) and involved approximately 80 teachers per school, four parents per teacher and 240 students per school. This data presented us with some difficult questions and finally led us to understand that the key to effective leadership was to be found in concepts from modern neuroscience and, in particular, in relation to our brains' locus of control. Lehrer's work was very helpful in this understanding. In *The Success Zone*[6] we combined our education research with concepts such as those developed by Lehrer as a way of explaining what we called the 'red zone'–'blue zone'

---

5   Jonah Lehrer, *The Decisive Moment*, 2009, Canongate Books Ltd, Edinburgh.
6   Andrew Mowat, John Corrigan and Douglas Long, *The Success Zone*, 2010, Global Publishing, Melbourne.

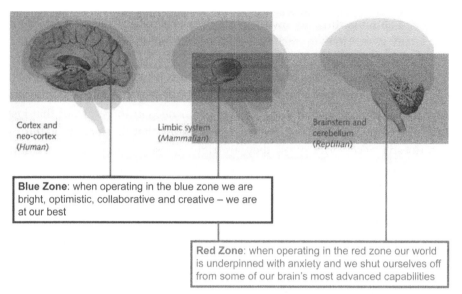

Cortex and
neo-cortex
(*Human*)

Limbic system
(*Mammalian*)

Brainstem and
cerebellum
(*Reptilian*)

Blue Zone: when operating in the blue zone we are
bright, optimistic, collaborative and creative – we are
at our best

Red Zone: when operating in the red zone our world
is underpinned with anxiety and we shut ourselves off
from some of our brain's most advanced capabilities

Figure 1.1   Blue Zone–Red Zone

concepts. Building on the underpinning of neuroscience we developed a shorthand approach for describing the brain's possible loci of control.

Neuroscience has found that one's locus of brain control is complex but basically centred in the combination of several brain areas. Mowat et al. called the reptilian-limbic combination *The Red Zone* and the neocortical-limbic combination *The Blue Zone*. In *The Success Zone* these are referred to as 'two minds'. These terms, 'red zone' and 'blue zone', will be used extensively in this book and are used with permission. The concept of 'red zone' and 'blue zone' is explained in some depth in Chapter 6, however, in brief they refer to our brain's areas (or 'loci') of control (see Figure 1.1).

When using these terms to describe the brain's loci of control it is important to note that they are simply a shorthand expression relating to a field of study that is very complex and still developing. There is much more to modern neuroscience than is implied in this simple model but, from the perspective of understanding leadership development from First Generation Leadership to Third Generation Leadership, these are the key areas of interest because they refer to the brain's possible areas for the control of our attitudes and behaviours.

When the brain's area of control is centred in the red zone, the emphasis is on survival. This is the part of the brain that leads to perception of threat (real or imagined) and so to the 'fight, flight, or freeze' syndrome that we see particularly in reptiles and lower level animals. There is no conscious thought in this. Life just 'is' or 'isn't' – it is not something of which the animal is consciously aware – and instinct makes us want to hold on to life if possible so we respond to threat in a way that offers the chance of living another day.

When this perceived threat is physical (for example we are threatened with violence or are in danger of being run over by a bus) then the dominance of the red zone is essential. Instinctive action is required and occurs. Unfortunately, however, because the red zone is dominated by the reptilian brain it is not capable of distinguishing between real threats or imagined threats and so it reacts in the same way whether or not a threat actually exists. In the modern world, a red zone locus of control can lead to some very inappropriate responses when a person perceives a threat even when there is no such intent from other parties and we see this all too frequently in some domestic, social, business, national and international events. Red zone locus of control also leads to the commonly encountered issue of resistance to change.

When the brain's area of control is in the blue zone we have the opportunity to see things differently. Because the blue zone is dominated by the cortical brain – that part of the brain which deals with thought, voluntary movement, language and reasoning (in other words 'with higher level learning') – we have the ability to see things as they actually are and to distinguish between real and imagined threats. This enables us to make a more appropriate response and to find ways of dealing with 'the new' in exciting and innovative ways. When operating with a blue zone locus of control we are better able to deal with complexity and ambiguity than is the case when we operate out of a red zone locus of control.

It must be noted, however, that this 'red zone–blue zone' dichotomy has nothing to do with our emotions. The areas of the brain that brings about emotion are common to both the blue zone and the red zone. In other words, it is not a case of 'red zone = unhappy', 'blue zone = happy', or anything like that. People with their brain's locus of control in the blue zone will have exactly the same range of emotions as they have always had. Any difference will relate to the way in which these emotions are handled.

What modern neuroscience has done is to enable us to add another layer to the leadership process. By understanding how the brain's area of control impacts on our everyday behaviour and by learning how to manage down the red zone while simultaneously managing up the blue zone we are able to take a new look at the whole concept of leadership and to discover totally new ways of dealing with the issues that we are facing today as well as those that will emerge in coming years.

In the first decade of the twenty-first century, we have encountered a situation in which the working hours of Western industrialised countries seem to be increasing. There seems to be an assumption that employees, particularly in 'white collar' jobs, should be prepared to work whatever hours are required to meet targets set by their bosses. Very often it seems that those in management and executive positions are expected to be available 168 hours a week (or '24/7') and to have no interests or involvements other than their work. In many ways we seem to have regressed to the situation that pertained over 100 years ago.

From reading newspapers as well as from talking with people, the impression is gained that many people today are scared of taking leave that is due or even of seeking medical and/or dental treatment that might be required because time away from the workplace could be penalised in the next round of layoffs or cost-cutting. We encounter situations in which companies crash, with employees, minor creditors and small stockholders left out of pocket – sometimes while directors, executives, the banks and other major creditors continue to receive their monies due or deemed due because of 'performance' clauses in contracts. In the event of non-executive employees seeking to protect their interests we are still likely to encounter similar anti-union views to those which permeated society in the earlier years of the twentieth century – the workers and their supporters are vilified for daring to want security of entitlements.

The French have a proverb which goes something like 'plus ça change, plus ça reste la meme chose' – the more things change, the more they stay the same. We need a new approach – something that is a real change in the way we do things. We need to move to a Third Generation Leadership world. But to reach this Third Generation Leadership world, we first need to put the entire concept of leadership into context.

2

Leadership in Context

One of the doctoral candidates which I supervised conducted action research into innovative ways of improving business profits. His research in a multinational company indicated that a key behavioural change by local managers, supported by their regional managers, could produce significant benefits in terms of both volumes of business and returns on that business. After using the suggested approach for several months a regional manager provided figures showing that, no matter what caveats they put on the figures, using this new approach was of tremendous value. The statement was made that this approach was revolutionary and very valuable. The regional manager then decided not to go any further with this approach because it would mean changing their culture and 'it could make other managers look bad'. From what can be ascertained, the top leadership levels of the organisation were not involved in this decision to reject the new approach.

There are many solitary activities. Leadership is not one of them. Leadership is related to the achievement of some form of outcome or result of individuals and/or groups.

Being a leader implies the existence of followers. How can you be a leader if there is no one to lead? It is the shift in the process of leading that is the concern of this book. First, however, we need to put leadership into context.

Some of the currently available material about leadership almost implies that leadership is an entity in its own right independent of followers. When I talk of leadership, however, I am referring to that process which is the hub around which rotates everything impacting on individual and group performance.

Some years ago a US-based company decided to expand into South East Asia. The company president, who was also the founder and principal shareholder, recruited local South East Asian people to get the new operation going. He appointed his son as the vice president responsible for South East Asia. Both the South East Asian operation and the parent in the United States thrived, but there was some disquiet among the local management team because they seldom saw their vice president locally – invariably they had to travel to the United States for meetings with him and he seemed to have no practical interest in anything other than lambasting the management team if it looked like 'bottom line' figures were in jeopardy. Still, because the local management team liked and respected the president, they smiled politely and said nothing when the vice president was publicly praised for the South East Asian results while, openly at least, their efforts appeared to be ignored.

A couple of years passed and the president made the decision to expand the company and a major European city was selected as the place they should be. The South East Asian management team were tasked with making this new operation a success and, again, they succeeded. In the third year of operation in Europe, the company president was interviewed by a major US publication. He made a statement along the lines of 'I am very proud of my son. It was his dedication and effort that made both of these operations successful. From the very start to today, he has been the one who made it all happen'. The publication was read in South East Asia. The local management team shook their heads and decided 'enough is enough'. First the local CEO resigned and he was quickly followed by the other executives and senior managers. Their statement to the president was along the lines of:

> What actually did your son do? In five years of the South East Asian operation he visited here 15 times and in three years of the European operation he visited seven times. At no time has he ever stayed longer than two days in either place. He didn't want to be involved in the planning. He had nothing to do with the hiring or training of staff. He never met with any of the bureaucrats and other centres of influence in either location. He has often been hard to contact when we needed him to sign off on anything, and we have never had from him any acknowledgement of what we have done – he has even opposed every request for any increase in remuneration that we have made or that has been made on our behalf.

The South East Asian management team knew that they had performed as required. They seriously questioned the performance of the one who got all the credit.

'Performance' is central to everything we do. We may define performance in qualitative and/or quantitative terms; in short-term and/or long-term time frames; of an individual, a group, an organisation or a nation. How we define it will depend on a whole range of factors.

In defining performance we need to appreciate that 'performance' per se is neither 'good' nor 'bad'. To some extent, 'performance' simply 'is' or 'isn't' – a person or group 'performs' or doesn't 'perform'. Of course the value set from which we observe such performance will impact on our assessment of 'good' or 'bad' – but that can be very much a subjective evaluation based on our personal, group or national value set, the time frame at which we make that evaluation, and, sometimes at least, on the pressure we are experiencing in relation to making an evaluation.

There are a variety of factors that impact directly and indirectly on whether or not desired performance is achieved. The process of leadership is what coordinates these factors. I am not getting involved in the 'what is leadership?', 'what is management?' debate as to responsibilities of those 'in charge'. I am using the term 'leadership' in its broadest sense to include what some might call management because I believe that, in today's environment, distinctions about 'leadership' versus 'management' are, in many ways, artificial.

Those factors which directly impact on performance are the 'ability' and 'willingness' or 'readiness' (or, if you prefer, the 'competence' and 'confidence/ motivation' or the 'capability') of the individual or group involved (see Figure 2.1). It is important to note that these two factors of ability and willingness are related but totally independent. There are many people who are competent to do certain things – they have the ability – but they are not prepared to do them: they lack the willingness, confidence or motivation to do them – for some reason or another they lack the 'readiness' to perform. Again, this is not necessarily good or bad – for example, all of us have the ability to do things that are unlawful: fortunately most of us are not motivated in that direction and so we can lead relatively quiet, law-abiding lives. On the other hand there are many people who will enthusiastically declare themselves willing to undertake

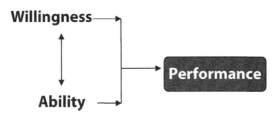

Figure 2.1   Basic Performance Model

any task even when they have no idea of how the task should be done or what the task involves. Such enthusiasm without skill has either the potential to be very good as some innate competence comes to the fore and they learn quickly or the potential for disaster if what they do proves to endanger themselves and/or other people. It is well known that the effective leader does not confuse willingness with ability.

An important aspect here is the direct relationship between ability and willingness. Generally (but not always) the more capable a person is – the greater their ability – the more likely they are to be willing to demonstrate this ability. Similarly, even if a person has very little ability for a particular task or activity, if they are willing or motivated to learn, there is a high probability that they can develop the requisite ability in a relatively short time. Of course, the reverse is also true. People who have been 'turned off' from education or learning or who are frustrated in their work environment are far less willing to develop new abilities or to demonstrate the abilities they already have.

It is this area that is the focus of most leadership approaches and leadership development programmes. The emphasis of many programmes is on the immediate leader–follower interaction and how the leader encourages a person (or people) towards achieving what needs to be done. There can be no doubt that these factors are crucial to performance and that they warrant the considerable attention they have received. This is a totally appropriate focus for one-on-one or one-on-small-group interactions in environments of low complexity. But the issue of 'willingness' and 'ability' is not sufficient in the majority of situations such as when a larger group is involved or where the leadership is being exercised in more complex situation. For these we need a more inclusive model.

The additional factors that impact less directly on performance are found in two areas – those in the organisation and those in the more distant area of the environment in which the organisation operates. (I must be clear here, that I am using the term 'organisation' to refer to any group of people who are working together to achieve some sort of result. Accordingly 'organisation' may refer to an entity as small as a family group or family business through to an entity as large as a nation.)

I will consider first those factors within the organisation – knowledge, strategy, non-human resources, structure and human process – that impact on performance (see Figure 2.2).

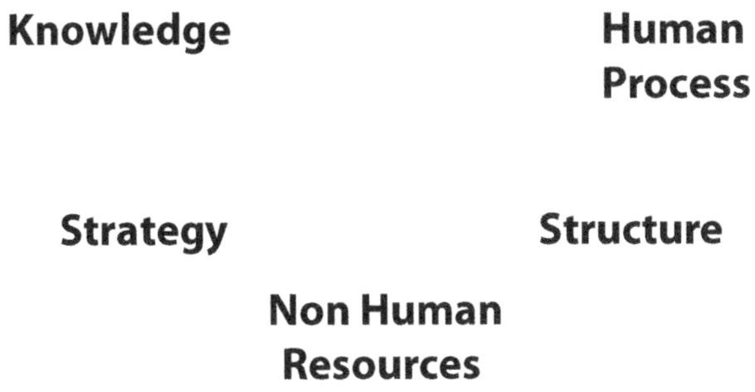

Knowledge

**Human
Process**

Strategy

Structure

**Non Human
Resources**

Figure 2.2   Internal Factors Impacting on Performance

'Knowledge' refers to the aggregation of data and information available – it includes the history of the organisation in a micro and macro sense as well as all the information that is necessary for the organisation to function effectively. Accordingly an essential part of the knowledge component is a high quality induction programme that links every aspect of every position with the vision, values and strategic orientation of the organisation. But this must be complemented with additional information.

Traditionally the organisational elders – the leadership team – have been the guardians of this additional knowledge and the ability to impart or withhold information has given these more senior people a significant power base – a power base that is often abused.

Many years ago, when I was researching for my PhD I became very aware of a misuse of this information element. I was studying the causes, costs and possible control of labour turnover and I interviewed the senior management in a wide range of organisations across several countries. In one internationally very well known company the person I interviewed was the vice president of human resources (a person who is now no longer with the organisation). Once he was convinced that the discussion was confidential and that I would not release specific company information and I would not allow any company to be identified, he was very open about changes that the company had planned for the next few years. Some of these involved making significant numbers of people redundant across the country. After I completed my PhD and was teaching back in Australia I watched with interest as the plan was implemented. With each round of redundancies that same vice president gave press statements in which he stated that the company had done everything it could to retain jobs; he said that, until very recently, the company had had no idea that they would have to reduce staff. From the public record of redundancy figures in that period, my total tally of the number of people made redundant proved to be almost identical with the numbers that had been given to me several years before. He claimed to be giving information. In fact he gave lies – because the company was implementing a plan that had been developed at a far earlier stage.

This information aspect now encounters increasing problems in some everyday but very complex situations.

Consider the issue of passing on information about the family 'organisation'. One responsibility of parents (leaders) is to help their children understand about their families (including the 'bigger' family history scenario) as well as the values and norms that dictate acceptable behaviour in the family. Traditionally this was relatively simple. One largely ignored the 'black sheep' and told about everything else. But today much of this information, such as family medical history, can prove to be somewhat of a problem. In these days of sperm banks and blended families there are additional complications relating to matters such as genetic dispositions and acceptable behaviour – the latter, especially if the children are older. An additional, but very real, problem in relation to this passing on of information (both about the 'family' and about life in general) is that parents are the fount of all wisdom and knowledge when a child is very young but, as the child matures, behaviour patterns become ingrained and the child's perception of his or her parents' wisdom changes. There is the desire by the young person to check things out, try new things, and to find other sources of information. Many parents have difficulty in dealing with this and family conflict may ensue. Parents often resort to various power sources in order to maintain their control – with the result that the child may well become increasingly disillusioned and rebellious. Wise parents – like all good leaders – choose their battles very carefully!

A myriad of other examples, of course, could also be provided about problems and issues with the use and misuse of 'knowledge' from the political or business worlds as well as from society in general. The example with which I started this chapter is but one instance of the knowledge factor receiving inadequate attention – in my opening example the issue appeared to be one of passing information up the line rather than the more commonly encountered disseminating of information to one's direct reports.

'Strategy' refers to the long-term approaches that are in place to help us achieve goals. It takes into account such things as our visions of the future and the goals that we set in order to get there. In commercial organisations (whether for-profit or not-for-profit) the issue of strategy is well known and usually well documented (even if 'strategy' is often confused with 'tactics') but in small organisations and families there may have been no real discussion or planning in this regard, which can lead to 'policy on the run' and decisions being made that are immediately convenient yet which create longer term problems. It has been said that many of today's problems arise from yesterday's solutions!

'Non-human resources' refer to the assets we have available in both the short term and longer term. These may include things like time, cash flow (in a family, monthly wages), buildings, vehicles, machinery and the like. The availability of these for the right people, at the right time, in the right place and for the right use has a very real impact on whether or not people are able to perform as required.

'Structure' refers to who does what and where everyone fits into the overall need to get things done. This is the aspect that draws together information, strategy and non-human resources. As has often been stated, 'structure should follow strategy' for effective operations. A key aspect of designing the structure relates to ensuring the non-human resources are available when and where required by those who need them. But it also deals with critical people issues such as discrimination. For most of our history there were clear-cut delineations between 'man's work' and 'woman's work', between 'young person's work' and 'old person's work', etc., and such delineations have led to many of the stereotypes and discrimination problems we still encounter today.

It must be noted that, in most organisations, there are two quite distinct structures – the formal one to which assent is given by everyone involved and the informal one which is the network of personal interactions and power alliances that has very significant influence over whether (and how) desired goals are achieved. Both of these structures are important and attention is needed to both if desired performance is to be obtained. I'm reminded of some more of Gilbert and Sullivan. In *The Mikado* there is a song with the words 'To let the punishment fit the crime – the punishment fit the crime'. It could be reworded: 'to let the structure fit the strategy – the structure fit the strategy'. (Although I admit these words don't rhyme and they are hard to fit to Sullivan's music!) Structure should fit strategy – and sometimes that might mean that neither the existing formal nor the informal structures are appropriate.

'Human process' refers to recruitment, development and the way in which people interact with each other. If the structure is appropriate then this sets up an organisation in which good, highly productive interpersonal relationships are far more likely to exist – of course, the opposite is also true. All people interactions are impacted by the value sets, attitudes, degrees of commitment, willingness to cooperate, and other 'behind the eyes' factors that affect how we behave. The human process factor is not only a key source of high productivity but it is also an area of potential conflict and can be the source of much that makes an organisation dysfunctional.

Aaron is an apprentice who loves his trade and who is acknowledged by his employer and his industry to be one of their best trainees. Because of other commitments, he is not interested in working overtime. His manager knows about these commitments but consistently tries to get Aaron to work late by giving him new work, very close to the normal finishing time, that will take several hours to complete but which the manager admits could easily wait until the next day. Aaron accepts the work but points out that he will be unable to complete it that day. He is accused of a lack of commitment to the company and of failing to respect his manager. Eventually he has had enough and he makes it known that, as soon as he completes his training, he will be moving to another employer. Effectively, over four years, his present employer will have invested a large amount of money in Aaron only to lose much of the return they should have received – all because a manager didn't understand the importance of the human process.

Or, in another industry, Barbara is a young woman who is part-way through her Diploma studies in early childhood education. She asks her employer for guidance as to the best way of assessing results of a project on which she has been asked to work but for which she has received no guidelines. She is openly ridiculed by her manager in front of the organisation's clients and feels bullied and humiliated. Because this instance of inappropriate management behaviour is not an isolated incident, Barbara then decides that enough is enough and makes a formal complaint about her employer to the appropriate authorities.

In both of these examples we see the 'human process' in play – and in both of them we see that, because the employer as represented by the manager does not really understand the importance of 'human process', the employee starts on a downward spiral of motivation and commitment to the employer while maintaining high commitment to their chosen trade or occupation.

Compare these with the case of Clara, a young woman who joins a large, well known company as a receptionist in the head office. The company, one of the most profitable in its field and a benchmark for its industry, pays well above award wages and has a history of caring for its people. It does little things that show interest in its people. It celebrates events such as birthdays, engagements, weddings, birth of a child, etc. by bringing the individual's work associates together and providing a morning tea or lunch and is generous in terms of compassionate leave in times of any emergency. Invariably the CEO is present at these celebrations and takes a personal interest in ensuring individuals receive support in cases of emergency. When Clara is recruited she is living out of town but is seeking accommodation locally. At the end of her first week of work she moves into her new apartment but, almost as soon as she is settled in, there is a fire and she, along with many others in the apartment block, loses almost everything. Clara contacts her manager to explain why she won't be at work on Monday. The manager then immediately steps in to help her find her temporary accommodation and arranges for her to get the essentials she needs. On the Monday, the manager meets with her, discusses the best way forward, and takes the lead in finding her new permanent accommodation. Clara is amazed at this response from her employer but, to her fellow employees, it is 'normal' – they see this simply as 'the way we do things around here'. Unsurprisingly, in this organisation with its revenues in the hundreds of millions of dollars, virtually every person gives the company their total commitment and works to the best of their ability. No wonder its financial returns provide the industry benchmark.

Each of these factors (knowledge, strategy, non-human resources, structure and human process) on its own has a significant impact on whether or not desired performance is attained. Together they have a multiplier impact on whether or not desired performance is attained. Accordingly it is critical that they are adequately integrated so as to ensure compatibility and harmony (see Figure 2.3). It is the extent to which these factors are appropriately integrated that determines whether or not an organisation has a positive or less than positive organisational culture.

Failure to adequately integrate these factors may well mean that no matter how willing and able a person or group is, they are unable to achieve desired performance because the system is working against them – the culture of the organisation is non-supportive. Leaders who have relatively low conceptual ability generally don't understand this. Invariably such leaders have difficulty in bringing about the appropriate degree of integration and, accordingly,

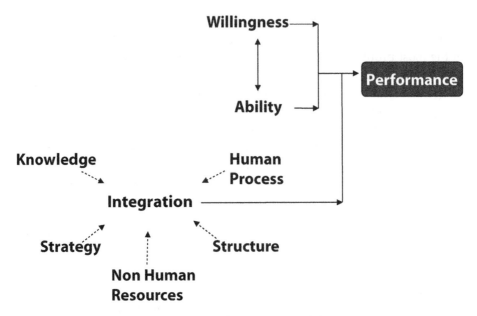

Figure 2.3   A More Complete Performance Model

changing the organisation's culture to one that has a high probability of achieving desired results through a committed and engaged workforce. Two examples illustrate the problems that can arise when integration fails.

A Sydney-based company gave the impression of always being very strong on dealing with obvious aspects of occupational health and safety. Issues such as keeping floors clean, ensuring no liquids on the floor, tidy workbenches and working surrounds, etc. received plenty of attention. However, following a severe storm in which many parts of Sydney lost all electricity supply for many hours, much of this concern was shown to be a form of window dressing. The power outage meant that inadequate lighting was available for normal work and electrical equipment (most of which was essential for safe working) could not be used. Factory employees were standing around talking – there was nothing else to do – when their manager stormed in. He demanded that they do normal work and threatened dismissal to any who refused to obey. One section of the factory heeded this command and attempted to do normal work or to at least look like they were being productive. Another section simply refused. They made it clear that they were not refusing to work – they wanted to work – but that they were not prepared to risk injury and potential death because essential equipment was not working and there was insufficient lighting to operate safely. The manager then endeavoured to start action for dismissing these employees on the grounds that they had refused a lawful instruction from their management. Phone calls were immediately made by employees to the relevant authorities. Only after the occupational health and safety authorities and the industrial relations authorities got involved did the manager back down. However, potentially the cost of this back-down was significant – there was the possibility that the company could incur very large monetary penalties for failing to observe safe working practices and for threatening staff who had legitimate occupational health and safety concerns. The company also faced an ongoing series of snap occupational health and safety audits from the authorities. Should these audits discover even minor issues that could normally have been dealt with in a low-key manner, there now was the possibility of these being escalated to significant and expensive items for immediate remediation. In addition, of course, any respect the manager had previously enjoyed from staff was totally lost and took several years to be restored.

Another costly effect of such a failure in integration was seen in the downturn of what had been a very successful company. Under the 12 years' stewardship of its then chief executive officer, the company had increased the net value of the company threefold (to well over $400 million). The company was privately owned and had a totally family shareholding through five trusts representing different branches of the family. The board comprised mostly non-executive directors with half of these from outside the family. A shift in the family power base meant that there was a significant change in corporate governance. Most of the existing directors were removed: new directors were appointed to the company and a new direction was set. All of this was fine. Such power shifts and changes of direction are not an uncommon occurrence in the commercial world. However, the new board then decided that the existing CEO was too close to the old board and requested his resignation. They followed this with an immediate and complete purge of the executive team and, over the next year, a complete purge of all those who had worked closely with any of the previous executives or who had been with the company for any length of time.

Within the year they had completely purged the company of anyone who knew the history of the company in any detail – they got rid of the entire 'corporate memory' base. The new CEO and executive team were very knowledgeable and generally experienced – but only one had any real background or any experience in the company's core business. They were all relatively young (in their mid to late thirties or early forties) and, understandably, they were very keen to show their business expertise and continue their climb up the corporate ladder – although most of them recognised that working for this company was simply a step on their corporate ladder climb. Within a year the newly appointed directors had impacted significantly on the knowledge, strategy, structure and human process factors – and the competition that had been introduced between the new executives meant that the impact of these factors was not integrated in any way. The company went downhill fast. Two and a half years after the new board were appointed, the remaining assets in the company were sold to a competitor for less than 60 per cent of its worth prior to the corporate power shift. Everyone was a loser – except the competition!

But apart from these factors inside the organisation, there are additional factors outside of the organisation – the greater environment. The environment, from a leadership perspective, includes such things as the competition, suppliers, legislation impacting on personal, family and business organisation behaviours, and a range of other factors that are 'outside' the organisation itself. These could include such things as building regulations, occupational health and safety legislation, anti-discrimination legislation, minimum wage and employee entitlements, the overall job market, international and national economics, and a myriad other issues that tell us what we may or may not do and how we may or may not do it. The Global Financial Crisis of 2008–2009 focused attention on these outside factors in a way that hadn't been seen since the time of the Great Depression 80 years earlier.

To illustrate the impact of the environment, consider the case of an organisation receiving government funding to provide important services to young families. It is set up to use self-employed contractors who are subject to police checks as to their suitability for working with children and it undertakes other appropriate probity checks on the contractors. The arrangement works very well for everyone involved and the service thrives.

If, however, the government in its wisdom decides (as they did!) that they will fund only those organisations that use their own employees rather than independent contractors some significant issues arise. Internally the organisation will need to restructure so that it has the systems and people necessary to administer a large staff and it will need to ensure that it has in place policies and practices that deal with issues as broad as occupational health and safety in the homes of their clients, transport for the carers, remuneration scales, and a host of other issues. The contractors will also have to make some decisions including 'do they want to move from the flexibility of self-employment (which includes the freedom to work for several organisations) to being a full-time, part-time, or casual employee?' The government's intervention has the potential to bring about the demise of an effective and successful organisation because contractors might not want to make the shift and it may prove impossible to adequately service clients. Here the external environment has a very significant and direct impact on the performance of the organisation overall and of the people involved with it.

In other words, whether or not desired performance is achieved depends on the individual, the organisation, *and* factors totally outside the organisation. The factors impacting on the individual and the organisational factors can be largely controlled from within the organisation: the environmental factors cannot (see Figure 2.4).

But even the issue of 'willingness' and 'ability' is a little more complex than is often acknowledged. Over the past 40 or so years the motivation industry has emerged. Today it is worth millions of dollars throughout the world. The motivation industry is largely based on the premise that people will be inspired to greater performance through stories of hardship being overcome and success attained. The argument is that people receive a psychological boost through hearing of what others have achieved and how they have done it: that this will inspire them to become similarly successful.

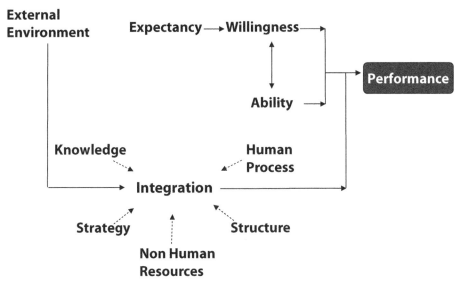

Figure 2.4   The Complexity of Individual and Organisational Performance

There is an element of truth in this proposition – but it is also open to serious abuse. There are people who become as reliant upon or addicted to 'motivational seminars' as other people do to adrenaline, gambling, alcohol, nicotine and other legal and illegal drugs and activities. These people require a regular 'fix' – generally in increasingly frequent doses (as can sometimes be seen in relation to sales teams where the majority of the remuneration is from commission on sales) – if they are to perform even close to the standards that are desired. To change the metaphor, some people are like campers around a camp fire who vary their distance from the flames depending on whether they are comfortably warm, too hot, or too cold. Without the external stimulus they would be uncomfortable, possibly miserable, and unable to function effectively.

Motivational speakers and motivational seminars can be a 'Trojan' within an organisation. They can infiltrate everyone's thinking to the point where it becomes necessary for continual outside input in order to maintain high levels of achievement. This situation arises because leaders either lack the ability to deal with complexity or they retreat from dealing with the complexities involved in facilitating performance and abdicate from their responsibilities in favour of outside parties.

Motivational speakers have their place – a very important one – but their use is often over-utilised to compensate for inadequacies within the organisation. Ultimately motivation is an internal drive. This was recognised many years ago by researchers such as Elton Mayo, Abraham Maslow, Frederick Herzberg and the other 'fathers' of humanistic psychology. It is also recognised by those organisations that seek to have long-term, sustainable performance from their people. These organisations recognise that, ultimately, the willingness of a person or group to perform arises from the expectations they have about performance standards and the organisation itself.

Most people want to do a good job. Most people want to put their very best in for their organisation. Preventing them are such factors as the quality and quantity of feedback and the stumbling blocks caused by inadequate or inappropriate integration of knowledge, strategy, non-human resources, structure and human process.

The role of the leader is to draw together all of these factors (Figure 2.5) and, by so doing, create a situation in which everyone involved can be successful – i.e. where everyone can both provide the desired performance and experience personal growth and development. Clearly this is a complex

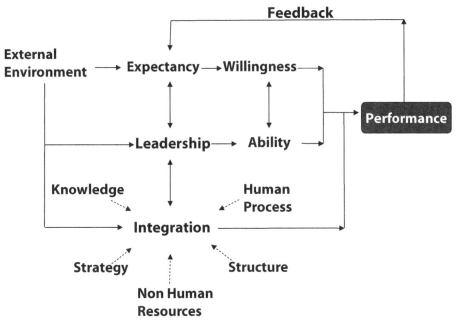

Figure 2.5   Leadership for Performance Model

responsibility and one that requires significant ability to deal with ambiguity and complexity.

A leader who is lacking in the appropriate level of ability to deal with ambiguity and complexity will invariably seek to reduce the leadership role to its most basic components (ability and willingness) and will concentrate almost exclusively on these. He or she will often complain about the quality of person with whom they 'have' to work and for whom they are responsible. This leader, pointing his or her finger at their followers, will almost always refuse to acknowledge that, when one points one finger at others, three fingers point back at oneself.

So far this is not too far removed from that with which most leadership researchers, theorists and practitioners would agree. Some may quibble about which parts of this are 'management' and which are 'leadership' but the general consensus would probably be that all these variables need attention if desired performance is to be achieved.

Under the traditional approaches that were extant until about 1980 widespread concern for these variables was not an issue. In the First Generation

Leadership world (see Chapter 3) only the leader needed to be aware of many of these variables (and they were probably less complex) with everyone else simply going along with what they were told to do. In the Second Generation Leadership world (see Chapter 4) again it was the leader's responsibility to ascertain and monitor compliance and, in the main, followers were prepared to go along with this. But the situation is different in the world of Third Generation Leadership (or Leadership 3.0). In today's world, everyone can quickly become aware of all of these issues that impact on performance and such awareness can impact on the motivation and performance of every individual – and hence on the performance of the organisation overall.

The critical personal factor relating to individual motivation and performance goes back to 'expectancy'. As I have said, ultimately the quality and quantity of performance for anyone has its genesis in the expectancy of the person and/or people involved.

When I was young 'expectations' were simple. Following the Second World War and through into the 1960s, New Zealand had full employment with jobs to spare and the question was not 'will I get a job' but rather 'which job will I take'. For most people there was little or no need to undertake university education unless you wanted to enter a profession such as law, engineering, medicine, dentistry or the like. Teachers and accountants didn't need a university degree – although many had one. In this world the expectation was that whether at school, university or elsewhere those in authority would ensure you received the information you needed and that they would develop in you the skills you needed in order to perform. There was also a general expectation that, during your working life, you would be employed by only a few organisations – there was some stigma attached to those who changed jobs frequently. This was the Second Generation Leadership world run primarily by First Generation Leadership people.

Under First Generation Leadership everyone knew their place in society and there was very little expectation that there could be any significant movement to higher levels. Accordingly the command and control ('you will') approach was effective. Under Second Generation Leadership the stratum parameters within which a person could move broadened significantly but it was still generally accepted that not everyone could have power and authority. Accordingly there was an expectation that followers would be told what they needed to know. Of course, for some people this was never enough and the phrase 'treated like mushrooms' (i.e. 'kept in the dark and fed bovine excrement') became widespread amongst those who were frustrated at being told what their leaders believed they needed to know rather than what was really necessary.

As someone once told me:

> *I get enough information to get me out of the muck once I've fallen in –*
> *but I never get enough information to avoid the muck in the first place!*

Arising from this, and an important part of the Second Generation Leadership world, was the matter of performance feedback and performance appraisal. It was recognised that most people were goal-orientated and also that progress needed measurement. It was generally acknowledged that 'what you can't measure you can't manage' and performance management systems were designed to enable managers to be more effective. The belief was (and is) that if you give people feedback on their performance, because humans are goal-orientated beings, they will then be inspired (motivated) towards better performance. It is a truism to acknowledge that, in the main, many managers hate having to conduct performance appraisals and most people see them as a 'necessary evil'. The result is that the feedback loop available from these is not often implemented as well as it may be and, far too often, performance appraisal, at least in commercial organisations, receives only perfunctory attention from all involved (apart from the HR team!).

But the situation is now changing. For those people who went to school from about 1980 the world is different and their expectations are different. We call these people 'Gen Y'. Young people today have grown up in a world where they know they can access information readily. Gen Y people quickly learn to sort 'information' from 'misinformation' and their social networking on sites like LinkedIn, Plaxo, Facebook and Twitter ensures that individuals and sources offering scams and/or misinformation are quickly identified and shared. Gen Y people are not prepared to be 'talked down to' or to be made feel inferior in any way. They are prepared to learn; they are prepared to 'knuckle down' and do the hard yards; but Gen Y wants to know that what they are doing is worthwhile and they want to be involved not only in what they are doing but also with the people they are doing it with.

Gen Y want to be engaged – and if they do not feel engaged, they will soon seek another situation in which they do feel valued and respected. The expectations of Gen Y are vastly different from those of their predecessors.

This shift in relation to expectations in Gen Y (i.e. those people born since about 1980), in turn, brings about a clash in expectations between the Second Generation Leadership world and the Third Generation Leadership world.

The Second Generation Leadership world (2G Leaders) wants to maintain a hierarchy in which those at the top have power and are able to use it. 2G Leaders are used to being able to control who knows what and when they know it – and this includes the right to provide partial or misleading information if they deem it the best approach in terms of maintaining their power base and in terms of the goals to be achieved. When 2G Leaders ask for input or say they welcome questions and discussion it is generally with the unstated proviso that no one will seriously question the 'what' or 'how' of that which is to be done – although they may tinker around the edges. 2G Leaders may see alternative suggestions as 'disloyalty' or 'lack of team approach' and they are very likely to punish (usually in a covert way) those who transgress the (mainly) unwritten golden rule that 'he who has the gold makes the rules'. A December 2011 article from Wharton Business School[1] places focus on this when it points out that many of the failures and abuses that have occurred in the commercial world over recent years can be directly attributed to the fact that the leaders of these organisations did not want certain matters to be discussed. When this happens, even if the prohibition is not explicit, fear of retribution prevents honesty and can seriously impede organisational success. There is strong agreement that leaders set the tone for the organisation. In this article Professor John R. Kimberly of Wharton raises the issue of 'a conspiracy of silence' that arises through inappropriate leadership and which brings about inconsistency between what we espouse and what we do. In the same article, Don Rossmore, a consultant in Los Angeles, makes the point that in any organisation, only those things that a leader really wants to be discussed will be discussed – anything else will be ignored or 'swept under the carpet'. There is strong agreement that leaders set the tone for the organisation.

All this is not something that fits the Third Generation Leadership world of Gen Y.

Gen Y works from the premise that authenticity is important – both in themselves and in their leaders. If there is a request for input and suggestions, then they feel very comfortable in giving such input or in making suggestions. In the main they are not interested in second-guessing the leader – they want to be authentic and they believe they have a right to say what they think or to

---

1   See http://knowledge.wharton.upenn.edu/article.cfm?articleid=2921

question that which is dubious, doubtful or unclear. Just visit any of the social networking sites such as Facebook or Twitter on the Internet and it is clear that these people are far more prepared to share information about who they are, their experiences, concerns and issues, and about what they have been doing than are their parents' generation. For those of us brought up in a First Generation Leadership or a Second Generation Leadership world much of this disclosure is at least discomfiting and often horrifying. To Gen Y it is as natural as eating and breathing – it is part of life.

Not surprisingly Gen Y finds rigid reporting structures and narrow sources of information to be a foreign concept. Their whole life has been lived in a world of personal computers, mobile phones, the Internet, social networking, and the like. They have learned that by using the Internet and the search engine of their choice they can find out almost anything about anyone at any time – and some of what they find out will even be accurate! Gen Y has an expectation that information will be readily available and that they will be involved in determining the accuracy and utility of such information. As I have said, their expectancy is that they will be engaged both with what they do and with those they are doing it with.

And herein lies a potential problem for leaders who continue to operate in a First Generation Leadership or a Second Generation Leadership world – including many of the leaders in the older, established religious faiths (as well as those in the newer denominations, sects and cults) in which compliance with their interpretation of what is in a Holy Book or what they believe is Divine Inspiration or '*the* way', is de rigueur. Gen Y sees as being automatic the right to question and to seek alternative answers. Unless they are involved in discussions relating to matters that involve or concern them, and can explore alternatives, Gen Y and many others today may well reject even that which is most worth retaining. The fighting of rearguard actions by those in authority – no matter what the sphere – only serves to further alienate those people whose commitment is actually critical to survival.

In late 2010 the entire WikiLeaks situation focused international attention on this matter of information. The WikiLeaks organisation had existed for some time and it is rumoured that it had been used by various governments to release information that may be damaging to other governments or individuals. However, when the founder, Julian Assange, announced that he had come into possession of about 250,000 secret communications involving the United States, the establishment went into overdrive. Politicians who should have known better (such as the prime minister of Australia) made comments that implied Assange was a criminal (despite the fact that he had not been charged with any offences relating to the leaks) and senators and others at the highest levels of US politics called for him to be charged with various offences (generally unspecified but including treason) or even called for him to be murdered or branded a 'terrorist'. Now whether or not Assange and WikiLeaks should have announced their possession of leaked documents and regardless of the content of the material (which is widely acknowledged by the authorities to have done little more than embarrass a lot of people and governments), the response is of particular interest. I believe that the response reflects an almost last gasp of desperation from those seeking to retain First Generation Leadership and Second Generation Leadership approaches – control by the use of information as a power base – in this Third Generation Leadership world.

I'm rather excited by this new Third Generation Leadership world. I like the authenticity I see – even if it is often confronting and means I have to make personal adjustments. I remember back to when I was a teenager and young adult. I and my friends used almost any subterfuge in order to do that with which our parents disapproved. The world of my youth was one where, in order to do what you wanted to do, but of which your parents' disapproved, at times partial truths were preferable and untruths were used if necessary. It was a world which clearly perpetuated the pattern of previous decades in which the only crime was really in being found out – and then, usually, it was a crime only because parental disapproval could be enforced by far more positional power than is the case today.

In this new world I see the seeds of openness and harmony. Sure there will be serious questioning of the status quo in every area of life including religion and politics. It may even mean the demise of some systems and approaches. There will be vehement disagreements and arguments. All of that is healthy. But, hopefully, it will be a world with far less hypocrisy and cant than the one my generation has made today. To understand how this drive for change has come about we need to understand the various generations of leadership.

3

Understanding First Generation Leadership

First Generation Leadership is dominated by the red zone and it needs the red zone in order to be effective. It operates under a 'you will' premise. Performance is obtained from an overt 'command and control' perspective (see Figure 3.1).

First Generation Leadership was the dominant leadership approach right up to the early–mid twentieth century. In this approach it was a given that you would become a leader either because of your social status, longevity of service, or because you had used force in order to overthrow the existing system. It is interesting to note that in this latter case, with very few exceptions, social status then eventually emerged because that which had been gained through the use of force became seen as being the right of the heirs. Of course this is the model that lay behind Hegel's Dialectic[1] in which an existing situation (a 'thesis')

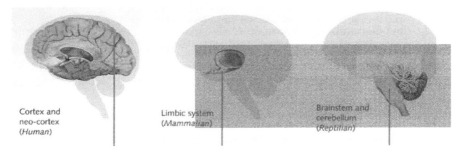

Cortex and neo-cortex (Human)

Limbic system (Mammalian)

Brainstem and cerebellum (Reptilian)

Obedience 'you will'

Figure 3.1   First Generation Leadership

---

1   There is a very good discussion of the dialectic approach and of what is known as 'Hegel's Dialectic' on Wikipedia – see http://en.wikipedia.org/wiki/Dialectic#Hegelian_dialectic

would attract opposition (an 'anti-thesis') which would result in a 'synthesis' which, in turn, would become the new 'thesis'. Karl Marx knew all about that model (or so he thought)!

Over the years (at least back to ancient Greece) a merchant class emerged to complement the power exercised by force and, for as long as can be remembered, power and wealth became intertwined. However, by the twentieth century it had become possible to acquire and retain vast amounts of wealth without necessarily relying on physical violence. As the wealth of the 'upper class' (those with 'authority' and/or 'power') declined in Great Britain and Europe, the term 'nouveau riche' became used to disparagingly describe those who had money and who were gaining power but were perceived to be lacking in social class – in the First World War, for example, it was not uncommon for senior British officers to make disparaging comments about officers who had gained their commissions by dint of a university qualification, new money or (like my Uncle Harry) were 'from the colonies'.

Because this form of leadership centred on the force (physical, psychological and/or economic) that those in charge could exert (or were thought to be able to exert), it was a leadership approach that was primarily 'command and control' *On The Psychology Of Military Incompetence*,[2] by Norman Dixon, is just one of the many works that provide some glaring examples of the disasters that occurred because of the unwillingness of (or an inability of) leaders to admit they didn't have all the answers and/or that, to achieve the best outcomes with the best use of all available resources, some of those they commanded should be consulted to provide input and expertise.

For First Generation Leadership to be successful it required a society in which everyone knew their place and, in the main, was prepared to remain within or very close to that stratum of society. If, as the leader, it is my role to command then you, as the follower, need to believe and accept that your role is to obey.

The Prussians were among the first to realise this. In his book, *A World Fit For Children*,[3] John Corrigan makes the point that compulsory education had at its core the intention to provide a compliant citizenry rather than to bring up our children and to enable them to think for themselves. He says:

---

2   Norman Dixon, *On The Psychology Of Military Incompetence*, 1976, Random House, London.
3   John Corrigan, *A World Fit For Children*, 2005, Castleflag Pty Ltd, Sydney.

State compulsory education is a late addition to the development process for our children. Initially, it was developed by the Prussians in the early part of the nineteenth century. The Prussians had been roundly defeated by Napoleon and severely disadvantaged by the Jena peace accord of 1806 and partly blamed this defeat on France's use of compulsory state senior schooling to create a cohesive citizenry. Prussian theorists believed that schools could and should be used to create a compliant citizenry, one that would be used to following orders, comfortable in submitting to authority and familiar with hierarchical chains of command. It was the Prussians who introduced the day broken into different classes dictated by the bell, a centrally controlled curriculum and teacher-controlled peer groupings of children.

This model was gradually copied by other western countries with the same intent to produce compliant citizens, useful to the economic and military needs of the state itself. You get a sense of its newness when you realize that it was only fully implemented in the last of the western countries during World War II and the school infrastructure that we see today was largely built through the 1960s, 1970s and early 1980s.

A little later Corrigan goes on to say:

Accurately, we can say that for most of history our children were brought up within the framework of community and it was their parents and other adults who shepherded them into adult life. State compulsory education was added rather more recently to shape adult behaviour and to transfer a certain set of skills that were of benefit to the state in terms of improving both industrial and military effectiveness. These were two, parallel development systems with two sets of objectives.

In modern times we can take the 1950s as the last time that we had a relatively stable community. Stable in the sense that people knew where they stood although they did not necessarily like it and it did not necessarily meet their full range of human needs. Particularly, society at that time was built around authoritarian structures and the belief in 'salvation through society' was still an organising principle of those who headed up such structures. As a consequence there were strong pressures to conform to the stereotype of a model citizen in a model domestic setting. Society's mores tended to be coercive and there were social penalties for those who chose not to, or were unable to conform.

A structure that would perpetuate First Generation Leadership in a post-feudal world was well and truly in place and, despite disquiet in some quarters, it was accepted.

The author Ray Bradbury[4] recognised the existence of First Generation Leadership and considered the implications of it in his novel *Fahrenheit 451*. In this book he describes a world in which books are seen as subversive and dangerous because they can cause people to think and to question the authorities. For this reason books must be searched out and burned because it is essential that society be totally compliant to the whims and desires of its leaders. Bradbury posits a modern world not dissimilar to the situation in the Middle Ages in which the established Church for many years opposed the printing of the Bible in anything other than Latin because making it possible for people other than priests to read and interpret the Scriptures could be a risk to the authority of the Church. Of course, some fundamentalists of various religious faiths even today still vehemently oppose broad reading or any higher level thinking and learning.[5]

There were, of course, relatively early reactions against aspects of First Generation Leadership – and W.S. Gilbert in the lyrics of *HMS Pinafore* is but one example. However, once compulsory education had become the norm and people were used to following instructions from those in authority, the system became largely self-perpetuating. In this world of compliance those who are older than me, more experienced than me, or have been in their role longer than I have been in mine, have authority, and I will be predisposed to listen and obey. When I am in a position of age, experience or longevity of service I will expect the same degree of compliance. I have a vested interest in maintaining the status quo.

This was the world of my Uncle Harry. It was the world into which, early in the Second World War, I was born and to which, for many years, I gave acquiescence.

In order to operate, First Generation Leadership needed formalised power and authority structures that would complement the work done through compulsory education of children. Fortunately such hierarchical organisations as the military and the Roman Catholic Church already had models that were

---

4   The first version of this was published by Ballantine in 1951.
5   Lehrer, *The Decisive Moment* (Chapter 7) has some interesting observations about this from a neuroscience perspective when he discusses the issue of 'certainty' of opinion.

capable of easy adaptation. These models made it clear that positional power was paramount and that the higher your rank in the hierarchy, the greater the positional power available to you. (As an aside, many organisations and faiths today are still trying to operate in a First Generation Leadership mode – and wondering why they often encounter problems.)

When I was in school (at least in the early years) we did a lot of rote learning. The emphasis was on sitting still in class and understanding that the teacher had all the necessary knowledge – our role was to absorb what was being taught. These were the days when 'obedience' was the key word in schools and, indeed, in society. Much of what was required from examinations and tests was the regurgitation of what had been given to you by the teacher. The measure of success was primarily the amount you could remember – and only secondarily in how much you really knew or could apply in a practical way and certainly not anything to do with you processing information and forming your own conclusions. We were at school because 'we had to be' and we learned what the system deemed we needed to know because it was driven into us. There was very little real attempt by most teachers to actively involve us in learning. We were empty vessels and the teacher's role was to fill us with sufficient knowledge for us to be able to fulfil our role in the stratified society in which we lived. (I know that New Zealand, like Australia, prided itself on being egalitarian but, in fact, there were some elements of distinction based on race, where you lived and/or the work done by your father.)

First Generation Leadership relied on positional power. Positional power in its most raw form is coercive force. Either you do what I say or you suffer the consequences. In schools (at least in my day) these consequences could be (and usually were) corporal punishment with a strap or a cane. In the workplace these could be the withholding of information, withholding of remuneration, withholding of promotion and/or dismissal – the last, for many years, without any severance pay or 'notice'. In society these consequences could be imprisonment or ostracism. In the religious sphere they could be excommunication and eternal damnation. It was primarily coercive power that ensured, after the end of the Second World War, that women returned to home duties and men regained the positions they previously held.

In a world where there were few if any safety nets to help those in need (such as pertained during the Great Depression) these coercive power bases were extremely effective. But even the safety nets that were available from various charitable institutions and benefactors maintained the status quo. It was still accepted that there would be 'haves' and 'have nots' and very often the charities themselves were coercive to the very people they sought to help. (As an aside, much of the 'Social Security' available today in countries like Australia and New Zealand still contains elements of this with such schemes as 'work for the dole' and 'mutual obligation'.) It was not until the advent of the trade union movement that there was serious, organised suggestion that the system needed to change. The opposition that was given to the early days of trade unionism (and still exists to an extent even today) was driven by a fear in those with economic and physical power that their dominance was threatened and that their lifestyles may need to change.

First Generation Leadership is egocentric – it is centred on what I as the leader want and/or need. As the leader, I am all important (or I should be) to you as the follower and the coercive power available to me will be used to ensure that I, and that which I represent, remain dominant. In this frame, my survival is far more important than yours and I do not want you to have access to people or information that might enable you to challenge me.

But it is also paternalistic. In this worldview I can help you avoid threat and danger by doing what you are told. I know what is best for you (because it is also best for me) and so I want (if not need) you to be dependent upon me for everything. This is one of the factors that lay behind 'company towns' – if you get your accommodation from me; if you have to buy your food and other necessities from me (or those of whom I approve); and if everything you do is able to be monitored by me, then I have control over you in virtually every part of your life. The old song, 'You load sixteen tons, what do you get? Another day older and deeper in debt!'[6] was an acknowledgement that some First Generation Leadership may be only marginally removed from the maintenance of a form of serfdom.

As we know, this worldview was largely accepted by the first generation followers. Class distinction was an ingrained worldview developed over at least hundreds of years. The industrial revolution had brought about a shift from basically agrarian economies to industrial ones but systematised processes such as compulsory state schooling ensured that the balance remained 'right', with wealth, knowledge, power and authority being centralised into the hands of the few.

---

6   First recorded in 1946 but the authorship has been claimed by several people.

But, by the 1930s, change was afoot. The carnage of the First World War had sickened many and the experience of travel undergone for the first time by soldiers who never before may have travelled more than a few miles from home, was having an effect. The lyrics 'How ya gonna keep 'em down on the farm, after they've seen Paree'[7] had a ring of truth that went beyond the physical experience.

By the time of the Great Depression there were movements to bring about a change and the Second World War added momentum to this. The era of Second Generation Leadership was about to dawn. By 1960 it was clear that a change in approach could be beneficial and Douglas McGregor made this clear when he introduced the concept of Theory X and Theory Y.[8]

---

7   Joe Young and Sam M. Lewis, 1918.
8   Douglas McGregor, *The Human Side of Enterprise*, 1960, McGraw-Hill, Kogakusha Ltd, Tokyo.

4

Understanding Second Generation Leadership

Second Generation Leadership has its locus of control in a combination of the red zone and blue zone. It is dominated by the red zone but accesses and needs the blue zone in order to be effective. It operates under a 'will you?' premise. Performance is obtained from a covert 'command and control' perspective (see Figure 4.1).

During the 1950s things started to change – very slowly – but change nonetheless. At my secondary school most teachers still emphasised strong discipline backed up by the cane but one or two stand out as men who sought to get students involved in their learning and who never had to resort to punishing students – to the best of my memory, Terry McLisky was one of these. (As an aside, by the end of the 1980s, at least in Australia, the use of corporal punishment in state schools was totally prohibited.)

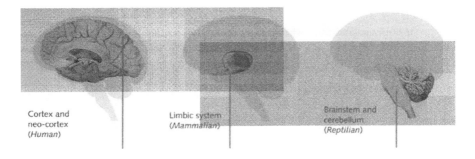

Cortex and
neo-cortex
(Human)

Limbic system
(Mammalian)

Brainstem and
cerebellum
(Reptilian)

Conformance
'will you'

Figure 4.1   Second Generation Leadership

By the 1960s the groundswell of change had grown and those in authority were horrified at the 'sex, drugs and rock and roll' culture that emerged in so many places. It has been suggested that if you remember the 1960s you never lived through the 1960s! At the same time management researchers were producing data which suggested that a different approach would be more effective in obtaining desired organisational results. The emphasis moved towards conformance with rewards for those who complied and the withholding of rewards from (or the provision of other punishments to) those who failed to conform. This shift was described by Douglas McGregor[1] in 1960 as the move from a Theory X approach to a Theory Y approach.

In discussing this period, Corrigan[2] says:

> In the early post war period we had a relatively stable community in which children and adults knew where they stood and adults knew how they contributed to the upbringing of our children. From the mid-1960s onwards we began to see the increasing erosion (or loosening, depending on your point of view) of this more or less stable community framework. Respect for authority figures and respect for authority itself began to decline. Church attendance began to decline along with participation in a wide range of other organised activities. Both the institutions of the extended family and even the nuclear family began to weaken with increasing numbers of marriages ending in divorce. Individuals themselves became less and less willing to engage in the activities that maintain the fabric of community, be these social activities, engagement in political activities or community activities such as community associations or volunteering for charitable work.
>
> By the late 1970s or early 1980s this erosion/loosening of community ties meant that the framework in which adults knew how to contribute to our children's upbringing and development had largely broken down. So our erstwhile adult in the 1950s street who knew how to act with misbehaving children, would act and be supported in those actions was now replaced with an adult who no longer knew how to act, or if he did know how to act was reluctant to act as his actions might not be supported. The children themselves may swear or act aggressively towards the adult, a parent might suddenly arrive and confront the adult or a passing social worker might suspect our hapless adult of preying on children. Under these circumstances the adult no longer knows how to contribute to the development of our children.

---

1   McGregor, *The Human Side of Enterprise.*
2   Corrigan, *A World Fit For Children.*

A number of factors influenced this shift that started in the 1940s. Among the most important were the growth of knowledge relating to psychology and sociology. As noted earlier, names such as Elton Mayo, Abraham Maslow, Frederick Herzberg, Douglas McGregor, B.F. Skinner and Carl Rogers[3] started to be widely heard and their influence grew. In addition, in countries such as New Zealand and the United Kingdom, unless you were in 'a profession' or in management, it became compulsory to join a trade union if you wanted to work. The voices of those who decried the perceived 'break down in society' as evidenced in the behaviour of young people were many and vociferous. Also, around this time there was an increasing incursion of legislation over what could or could not be done – legislation enacted as part of the First Generation Leadership extant at the time sought to do what society was 'failing' to do.

Along with this (and partly arising from it) emerged the study of leadership[4] as a discipline. Many of these studies challenged the First Generation Leadership approach and made it clear that virtually anyone had the potential to be a leader providing they were given the opportunity to develop appropriate knowledge and skills. By the 1970s the study of leadership had become a discipline in its own right and by the 1990s many universities and colleges across the world were offering programmes in which a person could major in leadership studies.

With First Generation Leadership there was no need for leadership training. Because life was controlled by rules and obedience was de rigueur, one learned these rules as one progressed up the hierarchy and there was no difficulty in applying them and enforcing them.

Second Generation Leadership was different. With Second Generation Leadership, leaders needed to learn how to bring about conformance and that led to the boom industry of training in and/or books on leadership. Use an Internet search engine today and type in 'leadership', 'leadership programmes',

---

3   Elton Mayo is best known for what is called 'The Hawthorn Experiment'; Abraham Maslow's 'Hierarchy of Needs' is a well known approach to human motivation; Frederick Herzberg is best known for his work 'One More Time, How Do We Motivate People'; Douglas McGregor is best known for his work on 'Theory X and Theory Y'; and Carl Rogers was the originator of non-directive counselling.

4   Included in any list of researchers and writers are Chris Argyris, Bernard Bass, Warren Bennis, Ken Blanchard, Jay A. Conger, Phillip Crosby, Peter F. Drucker, Fred E. Fiedler, Paul Hersey, Robert J. House, Robert L. Kahn, Daniel Katz, Rosabeth Moss Kanter, John P. Kotter, James M. Kouzes, Kurt Lewin, Rensis Likert, Barry Z. Posner, William J. Reddin, Edgar Schein, Peter M. Senge, Ralph M. Stogdill and Victor H. Vroom. The contributions from these and myriad others can be readily accessed by using any reputable Internet search engine.

'leadership courses', 'leadership training', 'leadership books' or a wide variety of other terms related to the concept of leadership and one is bombarded by literally millions of possible websites to visit. Obviously with this wide range of available material there comes an equally wide range of quality and there both have been and are people making lots of money through programmes of dubious quality. However, in the main, those programmes that are best known and that have stood the test of time are programmes of high quality and their users receive value for the money they invest.

By the 1970s Second Generation Leadership was alive and thriving. In this world the leader emphasised the importance of responsibility and experience and sought to obtain and retain people who wanted to perform. Respect was expected by the leader and the leader reciprocated by demonstrating respect to those who conformed to the requisite standards. Communication still tended to be one-way (from the leader) and extensive, open upward questioning was usually discouraged although, at least in principle, it was allowed.

The use of positional power and authority now developed from simply coercion. 'Legitimate' power (that afforded because of my position in society or the organisation), 'reward' power (the ability to confer or withhold positive reinforcement) and 'connection' power (the additional sources of influence available to me) became commonplace. The use of information as a source of personal power also became a serious contender for the most effective power base from which to operate. Of course, as before, the reality of such power was less important than was the perception of these power bases being available – for many people, perception *is* reality.

Another issue that emerged from these studies was that followers needed to have confidence in their leaders – and a key part of building that confidence was the knowledge that the leader could add real value because of his or her advanced conceptual ability. With First Generation Leadership this was not so critical. In a world where everyone 'knew their place' and in which obedience was key, independent thinking was largely discouraged as the manager would make the decisions and he (it almost always was a male) closely controlled the who, what, when, where and how of work.

Second Generation Leadership forever changed the world of management and leadership – even though many leaders and organisations failed to grasp that a change had occurred. Once the emphasis moved to 'conformance' rather than 'compliance' the issue of upward respect started to emerge. If I am being encouraged to conform rather than instructed to comply, I have the freedom to consider why I should conform – and part of that consideration includes the extent to which I respect my leader.

This shift has led to a form of 'smoke and mirrors' in the way we run organisations. Second Generation Leadership has become adept at using words and phrases that are sufficiently ambiguous to allow managements to do whatever they wish while maintaining a façade of caring and responsibility.

Where First Generation Leadership is egocentric (centred on what is good for 'me'), Second Generation Leadership is ethnocentric – what I should do is what is good for people like me ('us'). The important thing that emerges from this approach is the understanding of who 'us' are.

Many organisations speak about 'our people' in their value statements. I have watched with interest as many of these organisations then treat people at different levels in totally different ways. The issue of remuneration is a case in point. At the top level, directors and executives can receive significant increases based on 'performance' while those on or close to the basic wage are told that any increase is out of the question. The abuse of this 'performance' component was graphically illustrated during the Global Financial Crisis of 2008–2009 when the executives of some loss-making companies were still deemed worthy recipients of millions of dollars of largesse (usually paid out of emergency money provided by their governments in order to save the company from failing) even while those at the lower echelons were being made redundant and struggling to get appropriate redundancy payments.

While Second Generation Leadership has the 'talk' of inclusiveness, it very often lacks the 'walk'. Because it is a hierarchical approach that seeks conformance with the demands of those in charge, 'us' is invariably the people with whom I have the most frequent contact – my boss, my peers and/or my direct reports. Clearly the higher one is in the hierarchy the smaller will be the 'us' group. The language is sufficiently ambiguous, however, to allow everyone to interpret 'us' in as broad (or as narrow) a way as they wish.

Other language also impacts on Second Generation Leadership. During the 1980s and 1990s 'teams' became a buzzword and were often introduced as a panacea for all organisational performance ills.

However, as a myriad studies have shown, 'teams' – although a wonderful concept and potentially an extremely powerful structural tool – seldom achieve the synergy and results desired. The reason for this is quite simple. Teams, in the sense they are usually referred to in the business arena, are a Third Generation Leadership concept poured into the restrictions of a Second Generation Leadership wineskin with the result that the old wineskin bursts and teams become another empowering approach that is almost faddish. The effect is that either the concept of teams gets disparaged and dismissed or it is reinterpreted in order to maintain the same structure while using different words.

First Generation Leadership was a tremendously stable, long-lasting concept. It proved itself over countless hundreds (if not thousands) of years. The red zone of power; of command and control; of order and obedience brought both the best and the worst of the world that existed to the first half of the twentieth century. That is why it is often looked back at with a feeling of nostalgia by those in authority and this nostalgia, coupled with a fear of ambiguity and complexity, is why such movements as neo-conservatism and fundamentalist beliefs can still attract such strong followings. Unfortunately for modern First Generation Leadership advocates, the genie is out of the bottle and cannot be put back.

Because Second Generation Leadership harnessed the power of blue zone it is (was?) a transitory approach. The moment it became permissible (even if not encouraged) to raise issues and even to question authority, it was only a matter of time before the old model would be destroyed in its entirety.

Second Generation Leadership instinctively recognised that it was in danger and so attempted to take the new higher learning coming from the neocortical areas of the brain and subordinate them to a red zone hierarchy of power and authority. Such reversion to 'command and control' was (and is) seen consistently when leaders or organisations come under extreme pressure. Almost always there is a return to coercion and an emphasis on returning to traditional approaches in order to address new problems. The earlier mentioned example of WikiLeaks (Chapter 2) is a case in point. We deal with what Edward Deming[5] (the father of total quality) called 'special causes' because we can be seen to be doing something. However, as Deming and other quality gurus have made clear, special causes can resolve only about 15 per cent of the problems. If we are serious about resolving problems and preventing them recurring, we need to deal with the other 85 per cent – the systems causes. Dealing with the systems causes, of course, requires time, money and a willingness to make significant change in the way everything is done – and that threatens the very fabric of Second Generation Leadership organisations.

---

5   There is an excellent summary of Deming's work on Wikipedia.

As a result, the system creaks, groans and cracks with urgent repairs becoming commonplace. Restructuring, re-engineering, best practice, and other such approaches are used to introduce new language but, almost invariably, we maintain basically the same structure.

The era of Second Generation Leadership seems to follow a predictable pattern, as can be seen in the table below:

Table 4.1   The Second Generation Leadership Cycle

1	Economic forecasters predict possible downturn in the economy.	Board and executive team agree that costs must be reduced. All discretionary spending is reviewed and, later, stopped and money on 'non-essentials' such as training is cut. Advertising and marketing are reduced.
2	Economy moves into first quarter of negative growth.	Board and executive team examine the operations for further cost savings. Many good employees decide to look for new jobs before the axe falls.
3	Economy moves into second quarter of negative growth and there is, technically, a recession.	Board and executive team agree on staff reduction levels and redundancy payments. Voluntary redundancy may be introduced.
4	Retrenchments start; morale drops; quality drops; customer service/satisfaction drops; after redundancies are paid, ongoing costs are reduced; income remains static or drops.	Board and executive team bring in consultants from major firms to examine ways of remedying the situation. More cost-cutting and/or some form of restructuring is recommended and implemented.
5	Institutional investors become increasingly concerned as share price either remains static or falls and moves are made to replace or at least censure the CEO and other senior executives. There may be moves to replace the chairman and other directors.	Morale drops further. People are now working long hours and feel increasingly exploited but also feel cornered as they cannot easily find other positions. The number of people looking for new jobs rises significantly. Many of the 'good' people are recruited by competitors.
6	The recession bottoms out and the economy starts to improve. There is increasing demand for goods/services both nationally and internationally. Production and sales increase and profits start to improve. The share price starts to improve.	There are grumblings of industrial unrest as the unions now seek to get increased benefits for their members from the growing economy. Staff are recruited to enable greater production. It becomes clear that there is a lack of trained employees available for advanced tasks and attempts are made to recruit from any source, including overseas – this last step brings a degree of public outcry because there is a reasonably high level of national unemployment.
7	The economy moves into a growth phase and the company's results reflect the 'good' times. Imports and new companies take away some of the traditional markets. New products/services/markets are developed/introduced. Investors are making money from share movements and dividends.	Employment levels grow and new managers are required. The company invests in training. Executive salaries increase at a faster rate than remuneration at lower levels.

We have spent almost 50 years rearranging the deck chairs on the *Titanic*.

It is the knowledge that has emerged from modern neuroscience that enables us to now move forward. Of course, in doing this, we need to realise that getting rid of what we don't want is not the same as getting what we do want. It is critical that we focus on what we need rather than simply on moving away from an approach that has reached its use-by date. We need a new approach. We need Third Generation Leadership.

So what is Third Generation Leadership?

PART TWO
Live in the Present

In which we consider the leadership approaches that are needed today

5

Third Generation Leadership (3G Leaders)

There is a step jump from Second Generation Leadership to Third Generation Leadership. Third Generation Leadership is all about 'let us' or 'how can we?'. Performance is obtained from an overt engagement perspective (see Figure 5.1).

While First Generation Leadership is egocentric and Second Generation Leadership is ethnocentric, Third Generation Leadership is world-centric – what I should do is good for all people ('all of us'). While Second Generation Leadership was an evolutionary change from First Generation Leadership, Third Generation Leadership is a revolutionary change as it challenges the entire fabric of our traditional leadership and structural worldviews.

Third Generation Leadership moves us away from a world based on power and authority: away from a world in which hierarchy is accepted as normal and necessary. Third Generation Leadership moves us away from a world in

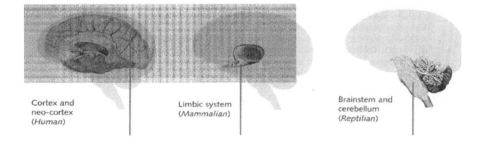

Cortex and
neo-cortex
(*Human*)

Limbic system
(*Mammalian*)

Brainstem and
cerebellum
(*Reptilian*)

Engagement
'let us'

Figure 5.1   Third Generation Leadership

which the leader knows best. Third Generation Leadership moves us away from a world of compliance, compulsion and/or conformance. It moves us to a world in which people engage with each other regardless of who they are or where they may be and in which they then engage together in order to achieve whatever performance is desired.

The characteristics of Third Generation Leadership and 3G Leaders[1] are:

- they engage with others as individuals rather than seeking to obtain obedience or compliance;

- they are collaborative and facilitative;

- they encourage growth and self-directed learning by everyone;

- they respect other people even if they are not receiving respect in return;

- they invite questions and genuine discussion;

- they ask questions with a view to helping others find their own solutions;

- they listen to help others engage with their own or shared solutions;

- they are totally non-discriminatory in thought, word and action.

Because of these characteristics, 3G Leaders are able to create environments in which people feel:

- emotionally safe;

- unconditionally respected;

- believed in as individuals;

- listened to.

---

1   In *The Success Zone*, Mowat et al. provide detailed information on how to develop these skills. There are also some very valuable examples and tools that can help in the development of both *Authentic Leadership* and *Third Generation Leadership*, available in Bill George (with Peter Sims), *True North: Discover your Authentic Leadership*, 2007, Jossey-Bass, San Francisco.

These are the critical conditions for people to be engaged not only with what they do but also with their fellow toilers. And the really good news is that, because these conditions are created by the leader's behaviour they are not some idealistic way of thinking. They are behaviours, and behaviours can be learned.

These leader behaviours create the optimal conditions for organisational and personal success in the twenty-first century – the conditions for achieving desired performance. But to get them, we have to move beyond the existing approaches.

One of the questions I hear frequently is: 'What makes a leader?'

Ask people today to define 'leadership' and there is a high probability you will get as many different concepts as the people questioned. Yet it always seems as though we all 'know' what leadership is. Ask people today to nominate 'good leaders' and you will get no commonality of response. Yet we all seem to 'know' the 'good' leaders in society. For more than 30 years I have been researching leadership by asking 'ordinary' people about their views. What I find is a bit different from what we read in many magazines and leadership books. The message I get is that a leader is 'someone who I can trust and respect and who enables me to get things done and who, in that process, inspires me to do my best and to achieve results'.

We need to ask ourselves: 'do the "leaders" we have today, meet this criterion?'.

Some years ago, *Fortune* magazine[2] in the United States made the following claim: 'Great business leaders ought to reveal all the traits of a great lover – passion, commitment, ferocity. Nothing less will do'. At about the same time, Professor Roger Collins[3] from the Australian Graduate School of Management said:

> it is difficult for CEOs, particularly for males, to disclose to a subordinate any stress or ambiguity, as it is seen in the minds of some as a sign of weakness, particularly by pretenders to the throne.

In other words, leaders are supposed to be 'strong' people who do not display any form of what might be called 'weakness'. A façade must exist that totally

---

2   *Fortune* magazine, 2 March 1998.
3   *The Australian Financial Review Magazine*, March, 1998.

obliterates the inner person together with all or any doubts or concerns that might be entertained. And when I examine most 'leaders' today, no matter what the area in which they lead, that façade seems to be very alive and thriving. I suggest that is caused because first, we draw an often-artificial distinction between 'leadership' and 'management' and, second, because most of us have very clear ideas as to what is 'good' leadership and what is 'bad' leadership.

There are problems with the popular concepts of 'appropriate' (good?) leadership versus inappropriate (bad?) leadership. These are, first, that we frame the concept in Second Generation Leadership terms and, second, that far too often we round up the usual suspects to ask the traditional questions. So, as in the *Fortune* example, the survey group comprised executives, directors, investors, shareholder activists and researchers. Dare one suggest that perhaps the findings were predictable? It seems largely true that a similar scenario applies when we approach 'the elite' (specialist journalists, commentators and academics) to comment on political or business leadership; or various social pressure or lobby groups to comment on societal leadership. The perception is dependent upon the point at which one stands.

How and why has the situation arisen in which most of us can design our own form of Procrustean Bed which then becomes the determinant of leadership (especially business and political leadership) and of who is or isn't a 'good' leader? Are the (primarily financial) measures of performance so loved by today's governments, boards and shareholder pressure groups still the sole or even the most appropriate means of assessment or are they indicative of a society in which the, purportedly now discredited, 'greed is good' mentality still flourishes? And if these are not the correct criteria for assessment of leadership efficacy, then what should we use?

Whatever answers we may give to these questions, virtually none of them will be likely to satisfy everyone. Almost always the criteria we use today are based on the fact that our dominant leadership models are still grounded in the First Generation Leadership or the Second Generation Leadership world – worlds which are no longer the ones in which we actually live.

In the Harvard Business Review's book *Leaders on Leadership*,[4] Jimmy Carter, past president of the United States, says:

---

4   Warren Bennis (ed.), *Leaders on Leadership: Interviews with Top Executives*, 1992, Harvard Business Review, USA.

[a leader requires] the ability to work with other people, the capacity to expand one's mind and one's heart as the years go by, and to see the broader dimensions of the future. Most important, it's necessary not to fear the prospect of failure but to be determined not to fail. If a leader is not willing to attempt things that might not succeed, then he has little faith in himself or the goal he seeks to achieve.

It seems to me that many leaders today are afraid of the prospect of failure. In my book *Leaders: Diamonds or Cubic Zirconia?*[5] I quote the people interviewed as stressing the first building block for a leader is for a person to recognise that they have a leadership responsibility and, coupled with this, to have the self-confidence to acknowledge they are not always right and so to have a preparedness to enlist help from others and to apologise when they are wrong. This openness to failure is a critical component of self-confidence – and true self-confidence is the base on which any leadership attitude or behaviour is built.

Most of us are born as outgoing, psychologically sound infants. Unfortunately some of us develop into introverted, insecure children and adults resulting in bullying, mental and physical violence, drug abuse, victimhood, a sense of hopelessness, and the like. The ramifications of such deterioration are immense and add to the many of difficulties society faces today including the increasing incidence of clinical depression as a serious all-too-common illness.

Most of this deterioration arises because we live in a 'red zone' dominated society in which personal identity and security seems to come primarily from obeying hard and fast rules and conforming to what 'society' deems as being appropriate. In this society a person's worth very often seems to be calculated by what they 'have' rather than by who they 'are'. The result is that most of us strive for greater material success and feel somewhat inadequate if we fail to achieve it. I suggest that the 2008–2009 Global Financial Crisis was a direct result of this approach.

We need to return to a situation in which a person's worth is based on 'who' we are rather than 'what' we have.

Self-confidence doesn't mean being brash, aggressive or offensive. Rather it means having a realistic sense of one's own strengths and weaknesses coupled with a determination to make a positive contribution to one's world wherever possible. Self-confidence means knowing you are a person in your own right – a person to be respected – and who gives respect to others simply because they

---

5   D.G. Long, *Leaders: Diamonds or Cubic Zirconia?*, 1998, Centre for Leadership Studies, Sydney.

are individuals in their own right, too. It means knowing that what you say and do is of value – of just as much value as what is said and done by other people.

True self-confidence becomes possible only when we shift our brain's locus of control from the red zone to the blue zone. Third Generation Leadership and 3G Leaders are conscious of this and learn how to manage down their red zones and to manage up their blue zones. They know that by doing this – by shifting their brain's locus of control – they will not only further develop their own self-confidence but that they will also help the development of those with whom they interact. Third Generation Leadership is open to continual personal growth in the leader as well as in others.

While physical growth is completed by one's late teens or early twenties, the 'expansion of one's mind' – mental and emotional growth – is possible throughout our lives.

The era of First Generation Leadership held the belief that those in charge should make and implement decisions. In this era we had 1G Leaders who then demanded obedience. There was little or no emphasis on most people continuing with formal learning experience after the completion of whatever schooling was prescribed. The elite would continue to grow but the vast majority were there simply to do what they were told. In the era of Second Generation Leadership, which held the belief that those in charge should still make and implement decisions, 2G Leaders sought conformance with their views and instructions. In order to get this, some ongoing education was necessary but the leader reserved the right to say what, how and when such education or training was provided as well as to whom such education or training should be provided. Again, formal learning was not widely advocated for anyone and everyone.

I have a sneaking suspicion that, in the future, historians may argue that the single most important factor of the late twentieth century was the explosion in availability of and access to information because of such things as personal computers, the Internet, mobile phones, and such social media as LinkedIn, Plaxo, Facebook and Twitter. When I was a child, most homes did not have a telephone and those that did generally had 'party' or shared lines. I remember when we got our first telephone – a dedicated line – and the envy shown by quite a few of our neighbours. My children grew up in a world where computers were becoming commonplace and my grandchildren cannot imagine a world without personal computers, social networking and mobile phones.

This is the world in which we now live and operate. It is a world in which young people find that most learning is done through networking outside of formal environments such as schools and universities: a world in which frequent changing of jobs is considered normal; and a world in which anything one wants to know can be ascertained almost instantaneously through the technologies available.

Back in the 1980s I remember one management writer using the old image of punch cards – those means of programming a computer or inputting data that were most commonly used during the 1960s and early 1970s – and stating that people now wanted to be treated as individuals; they did not want to be 'spiked, folded, or mutilated'.

Welcome to the Third Generation Leadership world. This is a world in which people are almost addicted to learning new things – especially if these can help them with social networking. This is a world in which people are very aware of the vast amount of information available and in which people have to make daily decisions as to what information to accept and what to reject. This is a world in which, fundamentalists of any form aside, many people are increasingly willing to grapple with complexity and seek new answers to age-old issues. This is a world in which we need 3G Leaders.

Helping others to develop true self-confidence and to expand their minds are activities that are only fully possible when the leader has moved away from the red zone of anxiety to the blue zone of courage. They are characteristics of Third Generation Leadership and of 3G Leaders. This blue zone of courage enables Third Generation Leadership to act differently from how leaders may have acted in the past.

Some years ago I was consulting to a major manufacturing organisation in Sydney. On my first morning on-site, the managing director took me for a tour of the factory to show me some of the areas about which he was concerned. Right from the outset of the tour I was impressed with the cleanliness of the place. Although the manufacturing process in this location involved lots of 'messy' items, the place was spotless. As we walked through it was clear that my tour guide knew all of the people working in the factory (several hundred) and could address them by name. That in itself was very impressive and, in part, it explained the obvious respect with which he was greeted by the people we met. What really impressed me, however, was when my host saw some rubbish lying on the floor. Having previously been escorted by managing directors and other senior executives as I walked through factories, I expected the usual response to this piece of rubbish – a quick look around then a terse instruction for someone to 'get that cleaned up'. This time my host surprised me. 'Excuse me for a moment', he said. 'Finders, keepers'. He walked over, picked up the rubbish, placed it in the nearest bin, and came back. 'We have very few rules here', he then told me, 'but one of our cultural norms is that if you see something that needs doing and you are able to do it, then do it'. He made it clear that this did not mean a person tried to do tasks for which they were not qualified or trained, but that, with things like rubbish, it didn't matter what your job: if you see it, you have the responsibility for dealing with it – personally. Over the subsequent weeks that I worked with this organisation I had myriad opportunities to see that this approach was adhered to by everyone. No wonder the place was clean, tidy, and had a very enviable safety record.

First Generation Leaders and Second Generation Leaders have a different approach. In a First Generation Leadership or a Second Generation Leadership organisation the problem or issue is seen by someone senior but, rather than dealing with it him or herself, an instruction is given so that someone else deals with it or cleans it up. How often do you see things like the start of a meeting being held up because a relatively junior staff member hasn't yet appeared with whatever it was they were supposed to bring? I have watched general managers and other senior people sit, wait and complain at the delay. A Third Generation Leader would go and see if the person needed any help or, better still, would have ensured that, if necessary, he or she had actually taken responsibility for bringing whatever it is for which they were waiting.

Or think about such mundane issues in the family as a baby with a soiled nappy (diaper for my North American readers!) How often do you see a male (usually the father or grandfather) call out to the mother that 'the baby needs changing'? Males can attend to baby's needs (other than breastfeeding) just as well as females. Finders, keepers! The same is true for virtually all other tasks around a home.

Of course conflict arises when Third Generation Leadership approaches encounter First Generation Leadership or Second Generation Leadership beliefs. Again, the aforementioned WikiLeaks issue (Chapter 3) is symbolic of this clash. But there are many other examples.

I recall a situation from the 1990s in which I was talking with the chairman, a newly appointed director, and the chief executive officer of a major Australian manufacturing and distribution company that employed some 2,500 people across five locations. The new director was very well known and had a formidable reputation for achieving results. The media saw this new director's appointment to this very successful, very profitable company as a sign that the company intended to do even better in coming days. I had been consulting to this company for some time and I had an excellent relationship with both the chairman and the CEO. I also knew the way in which the company operated and, I believe, I knew much of the reason for its success.

The company had a very flexible policy in relation to starting and finishing times as well as to overall hours of work and to the arrangements by which any employee could get another employee to 'cover' for them while they dealt with urgent private issues. This flexibility applied even in the factory areas. As long as the operation was obviously open during specified hours and as long as all key areas were always adequately staffed, people were free to deal with dental appointments, family emergencies, and other personal matters by liaising with their work mates as to who and how necessary task covering would be done. The success of this approach was seen in the fact of more than half of the employees having been with the company for 10 or more years. It was also not uncommon to see people returning outside of normal working hours in order to make up for time they had lost. The fact that this approach worked was seen in the high returns paid to shareholders and the premium international credit rating that the company enjoyed.

The new director stated that he believed the company employed too many people and that those it did employ were not working hard enough. He complained that if he called the company at 7:30am in the morning or at 6:30pm at night it was unlikely that the person he wanted to speak with would be at work and that, frequently, when he tried to call them on their mobile phone, it was switched off or diverted to a messaging service. He argued that by reducing staff and making everyone work harder there could be greater profits and even better returns to shareholders.

I asked him how the current profits and dividends related to competitive operations. He replied that, as I knew, the company was in the top 5 per cent of all Australian businesses. I asked him if the shareholders were pressuring the directors for even better returns. He replied, again as I knew, that there was no such pressure – in fact at the recently held annual general meeting (at which he had been elected to the board) the shareholders had expressed their total satisfaction with the way the company was being run. The chairman then, with a smile, stepped into the discussion and made it clear that there was no current belief that things should change.

Two years on that new director became deputy chairman and a year after that he became chairman. Within six months the CEO had been replaced and steps were afoot to institute tight controls in all areas of staff matters. Within a year staff levels had been significantly reduced and working conditions were strictly according to new policies set by the board. In the subsequent years, staff turnover soared, quality and quantity of output reduced and profitability dropped – and this was before the 2008–2009 Global Financial Crisis. Over exactly the same period the company's competitors in Australia were experiencing great growth and profitability. A Second Generation Leadership approach had triumphed over a Third Generation Leadership approach – and everyone was worse off.

There is an old quote that says 'If you love something set it free; if it returns its yours forever, if not it was never meant to be'. This is part of the ethos of Third Generation Leadership.

First Generation Leadership and Second Generation Leadership are very strong on control. In a First Generation Leadership or a Second Generation Leadership world it is necessary to know 'who is in charge' and to ensure everyone complies with rules and regulations. Freedom to think and/or act independently is seriously curtailed as was seen for many years in assembly line operations where, if a worker stopped the line for any reason (including a perceived emergency) instant dismissal was imminent. Only a suitably senior person had the authority to stop production – and even then he'd better have a very good reason! Mind you, this hasn't totally changed. As recently as early 2012 the Sydney media reported that an employee of the city railways had been censured because, when someone fell off a platform, the employee immediately activated an emergency plan to stop an approaching train. The report quoted senior management as saying that authorisation should have been sought before stopping the train! With First Generation Leadership and Second Generation Leadership, compliance and conformance are demanded and only those who give this will last.

Third Generation Leadership is based on engagement. And engagement requires that people do things – that they follow the leader – because they *want* to rather than because they *have* to. Engagement requires that the leader has developed high levels of trust and respect with the followers. When this is done properly the followers become committed to the same course of action as the leader.

This is something that those talking about 'engagement' from a First Generation Leadership or a Second Generation Leadership perspective miss completely. 'Engagement' in a First Generation Leadership or a Second Generation Leadership environment may contain an element of fear – if I don't get involved with this there may be some unpleasant consequences. Alternatively, 'engagement' in a First Generation Leadership or a Second Generation Leadership environment may arise because I am totally wrapped up in the task itself – I want to show how good I am in this role or with this task. By learning more about this and by showing how good I am here I will improve my chances of recognition as a true professional or as one who is worthy of promotion. 'Engagement' in a First Generation Leadership or a Second Generation Leadership environment is almost invariably 'me' orientated. In most areas today such as education with its emphasis on 'student engagement' (which seems primarily to mean using better pedagogical techniques so that students are engaged with the content they are learning), in business with its emphasis on engagement with the company, or even in religion with its emphasis on engagement with the local religious community, when people talk of 'engagement' it is this type of engagement about which they are speaking.

Engagement from a Third Generation Leadership perspective is quite different. Engagement in a Third Generation Leadership environment is because people are first of all engaged *with the leader*.

This was the sort of engagement I saw when I toured the factory with the managing director who picked up rubbish that he saw lying around. This was the sort of engagement I saw in the company that allowed large degrees of freedom among all staff members to organise their work so that both the company's and their own personal needs were met. This is the sort of engagement that engenders a true 'team' approach because the emphasis is on 'us' and what 'we' are doing rather than on 'me' and what 'I' must do. This is the sort of engagement that brings about individual and organisational performance that is well above that which is normally expected. This is the sort of engagement that 'delights' customers or clients. This is the sort of engagement that makes an organisation truly great.

But to get this level of engagement we need to have leaders who have made significant changes in their own behaviour. It is only leaders who are sufficiently self-confident that they can risk everything that are able to engender this level of commitment – and you cannot have this level of true self-confidence if your brain's locus of control is operating out of the red zone. As Jonathan Livingstone Seagull[6] said of self-confidence: 'You have the freedom to be yourself, your true self, here and now – and nothing can stand in your way!'

If, in practice rather than just theory, we are to move into a Third Generation Leadership world everyone, and leaders especially, needs to confront some serious issues – and that's where the matter of neuroscience comes in.

6   Richard Bach, *Jonathan Livingstone Seagull*, 1970, Scribner Publications, New York.

6

The Brain's Areas of Control

One area of leadership that, until quite recently, has not received much public attention is the role our brains play in the leadership process. Neuroscience[1] has been examining all issues relating to the brain for some years now and, in modern neuroscience, we find the key that enables us to unlock Third Generation Leadership.

Modern neuroscience is still a relatively young discipline and, within this young discipline, neuroleadership is still in its infancy. To understand the various generations of leadership and both why they existed and why they were effective (which they undeniably were) a basic understanding of some aspects of neuroscience is important. To understand why Third Generation Leadership is now emerging and how it can be implemented, a basic understanding of some modern neuroscience aspects is essential.

Neuroscience in one or another form is very old. There is evidence that as far back as 1700 BCE the Egyptians understood that the brain exercised significant control over behaviour. Some authorities trace back to Neolithic times the practice of drilling holes in the skull in order to cure various illnesses such as headaches. Certainly during the time of gladiatorial Rome it became clear that some people who suffered brain injury also suffered loss of mental faculties. Of course, for some, particularly in the nineteenth century, there was a sidetrack into phrenology (how the shape and pattern of the skull was thought to determine personality characteristics and behaviour), but overall the serious study of the brain has ebbed and flowed across the years – fortunately with more 'flowing' than 'ebbing'. Common to all of these was an underlying belief that there were fixed connections between the various areas of the brain – i.e. it was recognised that there was a specific part of the brain for each of the

---

1   There are excellent discussions and general overviews of the entire field of neuroscience in most encyclopaedias including Encyclopaedia Britannica and Wikipedia. There is also a very good series discussing neuroscience at www.charlierose.com/view/collection/10702

life process such as movement, memory, sight, touch, hearing, etc. and it was assumed that connections between them were rigid and final. While we know that specific areas of the brain certainly deal with distinct functions, the belief that brain connections (or synapses) are rigid and final is a view that we now know to be not the case. In fact we now know that the brain has 'plasticity' and, as such, it is malleable or modifiable. This has lead to the term 'neuroplasticity'[2] now being widely accepted and, with this acceptance, the opening of new doors for helping in healing as well as new opportunities for helping each of us in the way we approach and respond to life's issues – including the way we lead.

The second half of the twentieth century enabled a quantum leap in brain science. Modern neuroscience has its origin in the 1960s and the technologies and knowledge that started to emerge then. At its most basic, neuroscience is the study of the nervous system and with the revolutions that have occurred in such fields as molecular biology, electrophysiology and computational neuroscience we have been able to get an understanding of the brain that was never previously possible. One of these new understandings is the realisation that the brain actually contains a huge collection of interacting circuits or synapses and that, as one circuit becomes blocked or destroyed, it is often possible to 'rewire' things so that normal functioning can occur.

One writer, the Nobel Prize winner Eric Kandel[3] describes neuroscience in terms of its function or 'task' to explain how the brain's activities impact on all aspects of behaviour. He speaks of the brain marshalling its myriad cells in order to produce behaviour then he goes on to suggest that the absolute frontier of the biological sciences is to apply that knowledge so that we can understand the biological basis of consciousness and the mental processes by which we perceive, act, learn and remember.

This newer understanding has helped us realise that there are various 'systems' that control us. In general terms we often call this control 'our brain' but it is more correctly referred to as 'our nervous system' because it comprises more than the brain per se. The nervous system is divided into the central (or autonomous) nervous system and peripheral nervous system. The central nervous system comprises our brains and the spinal cord – the control

---

2   There is a very good discussion about this, as well as some compelling examples, in Norman Doidge, *The Brain That Changes Itself: Stories of Personal Triumph from the Frontiers of Brain Science*, 2010, Scribe Publications Pty Ltd, USA.

3   Eric Kandel, *Principles of Neural Science*, 4th edn, 2000, McGraw-Hill, New York. There are also some useful discussions on this issue at www.charlierose.com/view/collection/10702

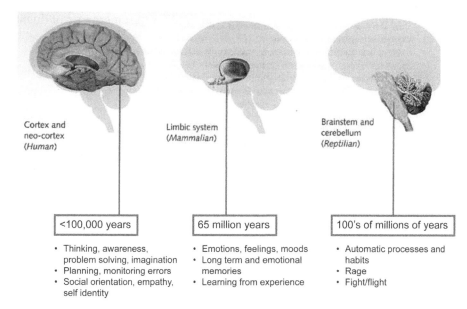

Figure 6.1   The Evolution of the Human Brain
Source: Diagram from *The Success Zone* used with permission.

mechanism and the transmission system. Jonah Lehrer[4] points out that some early views suggested that the brain consisted of various ascending layers and that the ultimate layer – the prefrontal cortex – was a complex overriding part that enabled us to be 'rational' and that 'being rational' was the core of being human. He goes on to explain that new research has expanded this view. In the Third Generation Leadership process, I am using a view we explained in *The Success Zone*.[5] My view suggests that, for simplicity of understanding, we can nominate three areas as illustrative of the areas that determine our brain's locus of control (see Figure 6.1).

The brain stem is a general term for the area of the brain between the thalamus and spinal cord. Some of this area is responsible for the most basic functions of life such as breathing, heart rate and blood pressure.

Another part of the brain, a fist-sized structure at the very back, the cerebellum, controls our movement, our balance and our posture. The cerebellum has been compared to a powerful computer, capable of making contributions both to the motor dexterity and to the mental dexterity of

---

4   Ibid.
5   Mowat et al., *The Success Zone*.

humans. Dexterity in both of these areas is required for the emergence of fluent human language.

The limbic system (or the limbic areas) is a group of structures that includes the amygdala, the hippocampus, mammillary bodies and cingulate gyrus. These areas are important for controlling the emotional response to a given situation. The amydala controls our 'fight, flight or freeze' response to danger and is the core of what I refer to as 'the red zone'. The hippocampus is important for memory and this area contributes to our ability to recall the past as well as enabling us to carry out habitual activities without conscious thought.

The 'cerebral cortex' is a grey-coloured sheet of tissue that makes up the outer layer of the brain. The thickness of the cerebral cortex varies from 2 mm to 6 mm. It is the part of the brain that controls our memory, attention and overall consciousness. This is what enables our thought, voluntary movement, language, reasoning and perceptual awareness. It is part of this cortical zone (the neocortex) that forms the core of what I refer to as 'the blue zone'.

As already indicated, some writers talk of these brain areas in terms that are inclusive of their various functions. These writers speak of the 'reptilian' or 'habit' brain; the 'mammalian', 'limbic' or 'emotional' brain; and the 'human' or 'cortical' brain. They argue that the 'reptilian brain' is the extremely old part of our nervous system and is common to all living creatures. In this model the 'limbic' and 'cortical' brains are later developments found in higher animal forms and only in humans is the cortical brain capable of full development. Research suggests the cortical brain is the newest part of the brain and this developed probably less than 100,000 years ago. Although these terms are not accepted by everyone, the simplicity of describing the brain's evolution from reptilian through limbic to cortical can be a helpful shorthand labelling in this discussion of leadership and the brain's locus of control.

There is, I believe, a difference between our brains and our minds. Modern neuroscience provides us with tremendous insight into the brain. It has taught us that networks of neurons produce intellectual behaviour, cognition, emotion and physiological responses: but there is much still to learn. Modern neuroscience enables us to understand something about the literally billions of possible connections between the brain's component neurons and the way in which these affect our sight, speech, behaviour and all the other things that, as animals, enable us to survive and grow. Modern neuroscience also provides us with evidence that, in many cases, if one area of the brain is damaged, it is possible for virtually full functioning to still occur as the brain rewires itself to use new neural circuits. Part of the reason for this rewiring is that we now know that memory, for example, is of several types (short-term, long-term, faces, locations, etc.) and each type is located in a different (even if some are adjoining) place rather than simply residing in a single 'memory' location. There is not just 'a' specific neuron or closely grouped set of neurons that solely comprise our 'memory bank'. A possible weakness in this decentralisation is that it may lay the base for what has been called 'false memory syndrome' (a disorder not acknowledged or accepted by all authorities) in which, because of some complex stimuli, a person believes they can recall some event even though the facts make it clear that no such event ever occurred. However, the beauty of this decentralisation is that we cannot simply go to a single location and remove all memory through any form of surgical procedure. Fortunately the strengths of decentralisation in the brain outweigh any negatives. As I have said, in relation to memory, there is tremendous strength in the fact of the cells being decentralised. Although, so far as I know it is not totally proved yet, it is quite possible that this same decentralisation occurs with many other brain functions.

It is also quite possible that at some future time neuroscience will be able to provide us with additional, indisputable evidence relating to our emotions and, eventually, to every factor that distinguishes the behaviours of various animal forms and, ultimately, to what is the very essence of being human. Perhaps neuroscience will even be able to help us understand the platonic concept of 'soul' and other religious and quasi-religious concepts that are so integral to the belief systems held by so many people. But we're not quite there yet.

Much of that is yet to come. Yes, there are indications already about many of these from current neuroscience research but, so far as I am aware, the definitive work on our 'minds' is yet to be done.

Why is this overview important? In this overview I have tried to give a simple (but hopefully not simplistic) introduction to what is the core of Third Generation Leadership – the brain's locus of control. In considering Third Generation Leadership, my concern lies with our minds – with the combination of various areas of the brain that impact on how we think and how we behave. My concern is on our brain's areas of control – the brain's loci of control for each of us as these areas impact on our role as leaders.

An important consideration regarding the brain's loci of control relates to the energy the brain consumes. Various studies tell us that our brains use about 20 per cent (+/- 1 per cent) of our body's intake of food (energy sources) and this

First Generation Leadership

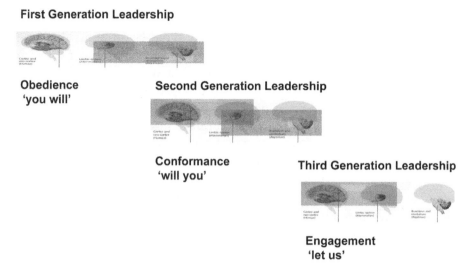

Obedience
'you will'

Second Generation Leadership

Conformance
'will you'

Third Generation Leadership

Engagement
'let us'

Figure 6.2   Three Generations of Leadership and the Brain's Locus of
             Control

amount is fixed. What this means is that a finite amount of available energy must be split between the areas of the brain that we are accessing: the more energy that is used by the red zone, the less energy available to the blue zone (and vice versa). This is why we can easily do those things that are habitual but usually find that it is quite physically tiring to grapple with new concepts – a situation that requires significant shifting of the brain's resources into the blue zone.

With First Generation Leadership the brain's locus of control was firmly in the red zone (see Figure 6.2). This is the highly developed, very efficient area of the brain centred on the brain stem and cerebellum. It is the area of the brain from which we do those things that have become habits and, once we learn something new (such as riding a bicycle), it remains embedded there and is available without thought even years later.

This deep embedding of knowledge was recently brought home to me in a very vivid way. I am a very enthusiastic (although not very good) golfer and for some years one of my regular Saturday playing partners has been a man who turned 92 in 2012 and who still plays golf three times a week. As a young man, A.J. (Nat) Gould[6] was a fighter pilot in the Second World War and, after the war, transferred from the Air Force to the Navy Air Arm. During his time

---

6   The combat story of A.J. (Nat) Gould is summarised in Michael Caulfield (ed.), *Voices of War*,
     2006, Hodder Australia, Sydney.

in the Navy he completed a number of parachute jumps and qualified as a parachutist. We play at Roseville Golf Club in Sydney. The course is very hilly in places but Nat almost always walks the course and plays off a handicap in the mid twenties. Recently Nat was trying to play a shot from close to the top of a steep hill. He overbalanced and fell. In consternation his playing partners rushed to help. In a controlled manner Nat tumbled down the hill towards the adjoining hazard, picked himself up, waved away the help, laughed, returned to play his shot and continued to complete the last holes. When questioned he explained 'once you've learned to parachute, you never forget how to do a parachute roll!'.

A further illustration of the complexity of the brain and the power of embedded memory was discussed recently in relation to patients with Parkinson's disease.[7] At a medical centre in Europe it was discovered that some people with Parkinson's disease, although they have great difficulty in walking, are able to ride a bicycle very successfully and there are moves to investigate whether or not bicycle riding might be an effective form of therapy for at least a percentage of those suffering this debilitating disease. While this is not totally 'red zone'–'blue zone' in the sense I have been discussing it, these examples show that when something is well entrenched in what Lehrer called the reptilian-limbic areas of the brain it is possible for it to then recur years later as an ingrained habit that can have very positive benefits.

But the red zone is an area that gives us only limited ability to explore options. The red zone concentrates on experience and habit – what has worked in the past and what has not worked in the past – and evaluates options in the light of this experience. Consequently it will tend to opt for either 'more' or 'less' of the same without necessarily exploring totally new approaches to existing and emerging issues.

The red zone is a vital area to which we need to maintain access. This is the area that warns us of danger and which provides us with instinctive ways for surviving. From a leadership perspective, this is the area that is operating in any command and control situation such as may be necessary in a crisis. You see it used in a positive way in such events as a fire or accident where the emergency service workers are seeking to deal with the crisis as well as ensure the safety of people and objects close to, but not actually caught up in, the event

---

7   This story is provided at various locations, including: http://btawa.org.au/2010/04/12/cycling-with-parkinsons-disease/_; www.nytimes.com/2010/04/01/health/01parkinsons.html; and www.youtube.com/watch?v=aaY3gz5tJSk

itself. Orders are given; action is taken; and there is no feeling of inappropriate behaviour because all those involved realise that the emergency will be best dealt with if there is a clear command chain with the most senior person being able to see and deal with the biggest picture.

The problem comes when this command and control approach is continued outside of the crisis situation. As has been widely recognised, if a leader is only able to operate in a command and control format, he or she might be a good crisis manager but the danger is that either consciously or unconsciously they will maintain their organisation in crisis mode because that is the only place in which they feel comfortable.

This was the issue that confronted First Generation Leadership once Second Generation Leadership started to emerge. It is also the issue that confronts fundamentalist and extremist groups of any sort. First Generation Leaders consider questions or differences of opinion as being threats. When a leader claims to want discussion and input from others but then ridicules anyone who offers an alternative or opposing approach from that which the leader has nominated you can be sure you are dealing with a First Generation Leadership situation. When a leader makes it clear that there is only 'one way' – that which he or she propounds – you can be sure you are dealing with a First Generation Leadership situation. When a leader maintains that you must accept that a certain book or set of documents are the sole authority in terms of what may or may not be done, you can be certain you are dealing with a First Generation Leadership situation.

In these situations full creativity, innovation, psychological growth and new learning are almost impossible in the follower (and the leader!) because they are stifled by coercion. As already indicated, this is the world envisaged by Bradbury in his book *Fahrenheit 451*.

The situation changes with Second Generation Leadership. Second Generation Leadership opens the way for higher level learning to occur not only with the leader but also with the follower because it starts to tap into the blue zone.

The critical differences between First Generation Leadership and Second Generation Leadership relate to the issue of respect, questioning and listening.

With First Generation Leadership, respect is not an issue (the follower automatically respects the leader because of his of her – traditionally usually 'his' – status or position in the hierarchy), questioning is actively discouraged if not forbidden, and listening by the leader occurs only at the discretion of the leader. Immediately the leader allows the possibility of a follower asking questions or raising issues, the situation changes. At this stage it becomes possible for the follower to engage in higher level learning because they have the opportunity to think about what they are doing, why they are doing it and how they are doing it. This is all blue zone activity because it needs the cortical area of the brain.

This ability to question and think provides an interesting dilemma for the leader as he or she becomes caught between the power structure of which they are part and the knowledge that obtaining input from followers may enable the task to be done more efficaciously. The tension relates to the extent to which the blue zone or the red zone is allowed to be dominant. Experience and observation indicates that as long as things are 'going well' the leader is comfortable with followers accessing their blue zones. However, immediately things start 'going bad' the situation changes and there is a predisposition in most leaders to revert to red zone behaviour – accompanied by a totally predictable regression to the red zone by the followers affected!

Obviously, in the long term, this dilemma is an untenable situation. First Generation Leadership could (and did) survive for hundreds (if not thousands) of years because there was no ambiguity. It was as though there was a sign at the entrance to every workplace, 'Turn off your brain when entering here!'. Everyone had a place in the hierarchy and for most of this time there was little or no opportunity to change one's status short of revolutionary activity – and the means for this were generally not available. But Second Generation Leadership gave some people the opportunity to use their brains – their sign was 'Most of you, please turn off your brain when entering here!'. Now, at least in theory, people were allowed some flexibility to think and, even if not overtly, they could question the what, how, when and who of leaders' decisions and activities. In some respects the surprise is that Second Generation Leadership lasted as the dominant approach for 50 or so years.

Third Generation Leadership resolves this dilemma. Because Third Generation Leadership has the brain's locus of control firmly in the blue zone (in other words, dominated by the neocortical area) the leader does not feel threatened by questioning or dissent from the follower and, simultaneously, the follower has the self-confidence to question or raise issues with the leader secure in the knowledge that there will be no punishment or victimisation. Under a Third Generation Leadership approach growth and development

Table 6.1   Comparison of the Three Generations of Leadership

Version	First Generation Leadership (1G Leadership or Leadership v1.0)	Second Generation Leadership (2G Leadership or Leadership v2.0)	Third Generation Leadership (3G Leadership or Leadership v3.0)
Worldview	Obedience	Conformance	Engagement
Mind state	Red zone	Red zone/blue zone	Blue zone
Leader emphasis	Command and control	Responsibility and experience	Collaborative, invitational, facilitative
Development	Disciplinarian	Expert	Facilitator
Professional belief	'Seen and not heard'	'Give me people who want to perform'	'Universal belief in every person'
Followers	Behaviour and learning managed by leader	Behaviour and learning partially managed by leader, partially by follower	Behaviour and learning managed by person (self-managing)
	Every person today can be engaged by a Leader 3.0, some by a Leader 2.0 and few by a Leader 1.0		
Respect	Unconditional, one-way (followers must respect leader)	Conditional, two-way (followers get leader respect if they do what they are told)	Unconditional, two-way (leader respects people regardless of behaviour or achievement, followers reciprocate respect)
Questions from subordinates (followers to leaders)	Punished	Discouraged	Invited
Questions from leaders	For the purpose of making a decision or forming a judgement	For the purpose of solving another's problems	For questioner to facilitate the other finding their own solution
Listening	When listener chooses and for their benefit	For listener to understand the problem	For listener to help other engage with the solution
Decision-making	Impulsive, instinctive	Intuitive, experience-based	Multiple viewpoints, analytic, team-based
How a leader feels	Superior when others fail	Responsible	Equal
Existential anxiety	Allayed by following the rules (life is predictable)	Allayed by conformance to norms and rules and confidence in learning from experience	Allayed by 'I matter to someone' and 'I am making a difference'

is available to both parties and, in my experience, both parties are very comfortable taking advantage of this in order to obtain optimal results. The blue zone allows for the full gamut of complexity and ambiguity to be explored and for new answers to emerge in response to otherwise intractable problems.

Andrew Mowat of Group 8 Education developed the table on the previous page to illustrate the differences between these three leadership approaches. Underlying these three leadership approaches lie the value systems and worldviews of the people involved.

7

Values and Worldviews

A friend was talking to me about an interaction he had with someone overseas. They had never met face to face but, over a period of months their telephone and email contact had developed into a potentially mutually profitable business association. While at a conference my friend had been talking to colleagues about this business possibility when someone made an ambiguously negative remark about the person and product involved. Clarification was sought but my friend encountered a total refusal to elaborate. My friend, a person who is fairly direct and open in his relationships, decided to clarify the situation and emailed his overseas associate summarising what had happened and asking if there was anything he should know. The reply he got astounded him, it said:

> your e-mail strikes me as 1) unprofessional, 2) disappointingly immature and 3) pointless. If you don't like my stuff, don't use it. If you do like my stuff, stand up for it and quit acting like a gossip-titillated schoolgirl … Take care!

Clearly there was a clash of cultures, value systems, or something.

My friend has a background in psychology and this reply from his would-be business associate raised in his mind far more questions than had the original ambiguous comment. As he remarked to me:

> when I receive an over-reaction like this – especially a personal attack, I tend to wonder where the person is coming from. We are clearly operating from vastly different world views when Jorg sees as an attack a request for clarification – something that could have been answered by a simple 'yes' or 'no' coupled with any explanation that was deemed necessary.

At the time of talking he was wondering whether there was a future for their business association. Whatever else may be said of this interaction, there can be little doubt that Jorg, the person with whom my colleague was corresponding, clearly felt threatened – his brain's area of control was firmly in the red zone at that point.

Value systems in societies are in constant evolution and development. As an example, it's not so very long since concern for environmental issues was a core value for only those on the fringes of society. Today it is far more central as evidenced by the fact of the 2009 Copenhagen Conference even taking place (regardless of the outcomes). We are recognising that there is degradation of our air, oceans, lakes, rivers, streams and soil. We are increasingly cognisant of the need to protect scarce resources. We are becoming concerned that the world we bequeath to our children might be a poisoned chalice rather than the great opportunity that was our own inheritance. Should our response to the environment be a critical part of assessing who is a leader? That is open to debate, but the leader's values certainly should be.

Is it possible that our business values have regressed rather than developed? Is it possible that too many of us have compartmentalised our lives to the point where, as seems to be the case with many political and business leaders, we believe one set of values applies in the workplace, another in society at large, and yet another in our personal and family situation? In a world which is becoming more interdependent and connected, are we suffering from increased personal isolation and psychological fragmentation? Bill George of Harvard Business School explored this issue when he talks of 'authentic leadership' and, following interviews with 125 leaders, he raised the issue of leaders in every sphere of activity losing their moral compass.[1]

Performance, leadership, value systems and worldviews are integrally intertwined. We will assess the leadership we experience and the leaders we admire by the extent to which we see demonstrated behaviour that is compatible with our personal values. We will develop and maintain our value systems in accord with our worldview. We will assess performance by the mindset that is triggered by both our values and our worldview. Our personal circumstances heavily impact on our perceptions. Unfortunately, for many of us, our worldviews are inadequate for the increasing level of ambiguity and complexity that we encounter today. The result is that our assessment of performance and our integration of the factors that impact on that performance are frequently far less appropriate than is really required. This issue of values has become increasingly prominent in the first decade of the twenty-first century.

---

1   George (with Sims), *True North*.

On 11 September 2001 the terrorist actions in the United States brought about a decade during which traditional freedoms in the Western world became seriously curtailed; the behaviour of the 'civilised' West regressed to the use of torture and extra-legal activity and, for many people, typified a clash between 'Christian' values and 'Islamic' values. This perceived clash, of course, was seriously wrong. Yes, there was (and is) a clash of values but it is not religious – the reality is a clash between narrow, fundamentalist values and a freer, cosmopolitan and inclusive worldview: a clash between those who want to retain a First Generation Leadership world on their terms and those who reject those particular terms – and that has nothing whatsoever to do with race, religion or anything else – it is far more a matter of the extent to which our brains are red zone or blue zone controlled. In the red zone our whole approach is underpinned by anxiety and fear (see Figure 1.1 on page 14).

In the first four months of 2011 there were uprisings against the status quo in Tunisia, Egypt, Syria, Bahrain, Libya and other countries. In Tunisia and Egypt the rulers were deposed relatively quickly and with a reasonably small amount of violence and loss of life. In other places the rulers resisted any move for change and came down heavily on those who dared to question the status quo. One of the factors that impacted on these uprisings was the range of social media available on computers and mobile phones. Accounts of what was happening (both words and pictures) flashed around the world and some of the countries affected (as well as many countries where those in power feared that the call for change could extend further) sought to shut down social networking so as to limit the ability of people to coordinate their resistance. Again and again ordinary people were saying 'we need to move away from a repressive, controlling system of government that is intent on maintaining power and authority in the hands of the few. We need a new form government: of leadership'. Values had changed for many people while their governments and rulers wanted to retain the values from the past.

Some years ago the late Professor Clare Graves[2] suggested an open-ended spiral of worldviews to explain why, so often, problems occur and/or people respond in an inadequate fashion to issues they encounter. Graves was in many ways one of the pioneers in some aspects of modern neuroscience thought (although he is not generally acknowledged for this) and he argued that humans move in their worldviews from instinct, through safety, power,

---

2 Details of Graves' work are set out in D. Beck and C. Cowan, *Spiral Dynamics: Mastering Values, Leadership and Change*, 1996, Blackwell Publishers Inc., USA and in D. Lynch and Paul L. Kordis, *Strategy of the Dolphin*, 1990, Ballantine Books, USA.

order, success, people, process and synthesis approaches – that there is plasticity in the brain in relation to how we view the world and respond to it. These worldviews represent rising levels of openness and ability to deal with complexity and ambiguity. For the first six of these a person can see only that approach (effectively a monochromatic perspective) while they are in that worldview and this temporarily limits the options they consider when dealing with any issue.[3] So, as an example, for a person operating out of what Graves terms the level of family or tribe, options will be considered in relation to those people I consider 'mine' and any detrimental impact on others will be of little or no concern. Only at the process or integrated systems level (Graves' second tier) does a polychromatic perspective become possible so that a greater variety of options become apparent. In other words, only at the process level does a person become fully willing and able to consider in depth options that involve greater levels of ambiguity and complexity in relation to resolving otherwise intractable problems. Only at the process level and above can a person more appropriately choose how and when they use different worldviews.

Under Graves' concepts, during their lifetime a person develops (or not) along a spiral depending on their response to things they encounter. When they realise that their current worldview is failing to provide the solutions they need, a person can choose to stop where they are, pause and consider before taking action, or make the move freely to the next stage. At any point the person continues to have access to, and to use, the earlier stages of the spiral – the important thing is to understand the strengths and limitations of each stage and, as much as possible, to access them appropriately. Graves' approach can be summarised in the table opposite.[4]

The dominant worldview of virtually all societies for many years has been a Level 1.4 value system in which rules and regulations (do it my way) are extant. This worldview is backed up by the Level 1.3 value system of power in which there can be severe punishments for those who resist or who seek a different way. It is this worldview that has been (and is) the driver of empire and conquest (the world's policeman?) and which, in many ways, is responsible for both the best and the worst of what exists today in every sphere of human endeavour. The indication that a change may be necessary always starts with

---

3   An interesting neuroscience perspective on this can be found in B.E. Wexler, *Brain and Culture: Neurobiology, Ideology, and Social Change*, 2006, MIT Press, Cambridge, MA, where he discusses the difficulty we have in changing our 'usual' response when confronted by information that doesn't match our beliefs or worldviews.
4   This table is an adaptation of a presentation by Don Beck and Chris Cowan of the National Values Centre during a workshop on Spiral Dynamics in 1997.

Table 7.1 Stages of Human Development – Clare Graves

Identification	Common characteristics and value system	Identifying slogan
Level 1.1	Purely animalistic survival. Individual survival is paramount. Found very seldom in society except in babies and very ill people who have regressed to infantile states.	'I will survive at the most basic level'
Level 1.2	A concern for other worldly powers which might be found in traditional religions or in astrology, new age concepts such as crystals, the occult, etc. People are bonded in an almost tribal fashion depending on their adherence to the particular belief system, but follow and have allegiance to the chief or elder. This is also the level that bonds together a close family or group such as may be seen in a religious community.	'The family that prays together stays together'
Level 1.3	Aggressively seeking what is wanted, *NOW*. No guilt and or sense of commitment except to those who are 'on my side' and support me. The most powerful person becomes the leader and allegiance is based on having and holding power. Seen extensively in gangs and much antisocial individualistic behaviour. Money and other commodities are pursued for their power component rather than for themselves. On the positive side, this indicates risk takers, entrepreneurs, explorers, researchers breaking new ground, etc.	'Might is right' 'Kick the door in' 'Make it happen'
Level 1.4	At this level, people recognise the need for and value of law and order. Everything has a place and everything should be done decently and in order. Those who adhere to the 'right way' are assured of benefits in the future with the result that delayed gratification is acceptable. A person can 'put up' with all sorts of perceived injustices because 'that's the rule' and, in the long term, things will even out. This level also supports perfection, craftsmen, conservatism, skill development, and is used by coaches, teachers, lawyers and police.	'This is the way. Walk ye in it' 'Keeps me safe'
Level 1.5	Competition is both good and necessary. We should strive to encourage individual responsibility and individual wealth. Ultimately the weak should go to the wall, as market forces should dictate what survives and distribution of wealth. Economic rationalism is paramount and we encourage people to look after their own education, health services, retirement, etc. This level also provides a better life, rewards risk takers, seeks alternatives as the better way, etc.	'Greed is good' 'Things can be better'

Table 7.1 Continued

Identification	Common characteristics and value system	Identifying slogan
Level 1.6	The attainment of material gains is, ultimately, self-destructive. 'Vanity of vanities', saith the preacher, 'all is vanity'. We have a responsibility that is beyond ourselves to the socially and economically disadvantaged as well as to those who are powerless to care for themselves in our world – whales, oceans, the ozone layer, forests, etc. We should be concerned about the world we are bequeathing to our children and our children's children. This level also works for the growth of teams, seeks equality, and works for the end of 'isms' such as racism, sexism, ageism, etc.	'We must be socially responsible'
Level 2.1	This level is a quantum leap from the previous approach and is the first level at which all preceding levels are truly seen as 'just different'. People operating primarily at this level are able to recognise and use all preceding levels of complexity as valid and useful tools and/or understandings of the way by which humanity confronts and deals with the life conditions we encounter.	'Lets look at the total system'
Level 2.2	Understanding of this is still developing and there are very few (if any) proven examples of extensive Level 2.2 thinking. It appears to recognise the reality of powers and forces that are beyond our understanding but these are seen simply as gaps in our knowledge rather than mysterious 'other' such as would be believed by people operating primarily from a Level 1.2 system.	'An holistic view'

disquiet about the status quo – a belief that things could be different from what they are and that today's problems may be capable of solution if we approach them in a different way. I believe that it is this disquiet that we are seeing today.

Of course this doesn't mean that the people in these countries experiencing 'the Arab Spring' are moving to a Third Generation Leadership world. What it does mean, however, is that their current leadership world is failing to meet their needs. This 'dissatisfaction quotient' is equally true for the Al-Qaeda phenomenon as it is for the current unrest in Middle Eastern countries. The late, mostly unlamented, Osama Bin Laden wanted the United States and other Western powers to get out of all Muslim countries and was prepared to use terrorism in quest of this aim – but what he wanted was to install another regime – he was not seeking a world in which there would be unconditional respect for each person and in which listening and engagement would be the norm. I suspect that at least some of his followers, while fully supporting his first aim, failed to appreciate the implications of his second. What many people fail to realise, at least initially, is that getting rid of what you don't want is quite different from getting what you do want.

Unsurprisingly there are similarities here with the 'red zone'–'blue zone' area of brain control concepts. As a baby grows and develops through childhood into adulthood, his or her overall brain develops from a purely instinctive 'stimulus-response' organ to one that is capable of great learning and achievement. In a mature adult the neofrontal cortex is fully developed and accessible even if we don't always allow it to control how we think and act. In times of extreme danger such as the possibility of being hit by a vehicle, an instinctive jump for safety (basic brain response) is totally appropriate. However, for more complex situations, if we have a greater degree of flexibility in response available to us we are more likely to make an appropriate decision – and that requires blue zone activation. However, some people become stuck in a primarily red zone area of control (even when at least part of their worldview may be at the second tier) and that can result in continuously inappropriate behaviour and poor decisions.

This evolution of worldviews and values impacts every part of life. In theory, the world in which we bring up our children today is vastly better than the one that our forefathers knew. And, again in theory, our children's children will live in an even better world than that of today.

I suggest, however, reality shows that in many ways what happens in our world is not as different from the past as we might hope. This is because our dominant societal view tends to be centred at too low a level on Graves' Spiral and, as a consequence, we are almost 'locked into' a red zone approach.

Yes, we have a greater life expectancy today than ever before – at least for non-indigenous people in the Western world. Yes, we have the technological ability to feed, house and clothe every person in the world at a very satisfactory level – yet most of our technology is used for military purposes (coercive power) or to increase power and wealth for a minority of the world's people. Yes, we have medicine and drugs that could alleviate or cure much of the suffering people experience – yet we price these in such a way that the poorest countries and people cannot access them.

We are caught in a dilemma that is as old as humanity itself. On one side is the drive for fulfilling one's potential and achieving both economic success and happiness. On the other side is the drive to care for those people less fortunate than we are and to provide a better world for them as well as for us. Our rhetoric says that, if we improve things for ourselves, this will then have a flow-on effect of improving things for them. Unfortunately practice shows that as many of us gain personal and economic success we tend to forget the rhetoric.

A simple recapping of the history of management thought over the twentieth century illustrates this. At the turn of the twentieth century there were little or no generally accepted 'management' practices. The worst evils of child exploitation and slavery had been abolished in Europe, the United States, and most other countries. But working conditions were still reasonably poor. There was little or no legislation on occupational health and safety. Workers had little or no protection from exploitative employers. The drive was to produce goods and services at the lowest cost while selling them at the highest price. Care for the environment was largely ignored. The wealthy and the powerful saw a world that was theirs for the exploiting – and they took advantage of every opportunity to do just that. Graves' Level 1.3 (power rules) view of the world was alive and well.

Then, for 20 or so years the emphasis of management was on efficiency. The challenge was to produce things in the most cost-effective way and to help in this 'time and motion' studies were used for the removal of inefficient practices. The invention of the assembly line was a logical extension of these studies although it often engendered a situation in which the assembly line itself was of greater importance than the people who worked on it. Graves' Level 1.4 (legalistic or observe the rules) view of the world was starting to emerge in strength.

The 'Great Depression' which preceded the Second World War brought an end to some of the excesses that had developed and, around this time, there was a move to recognise the importance of people. By the 1950s the study of 'management' as a discipline in its own right was well established and the literature was arguing for a humanistic approach. There was recognition that the people who worked in organisations had rights and that, in the quest for production and sale of goods and services, these rights could not be ignored. From here it was but a small step to the establishment of 'personnel' services (more recently known as 'Human Resources') as a subset of management and, eventually, as a key department in most organisational structures. Graves' Level 1.4 (legalistic or observe the rules) view of the world was dominant but tempered by both Level 1.2 (family or tribe) and Level 1.6 (concern for others) perspectives.

By the 1970s, at least in the Western industrialised countries, there was a creative tension between concern for people and concern for production. Organisations sought to produce their goods and services with people who were well trained and, in the main, reasonably recompensed for their services. The gap between remuneration at the top and bottom of organisations certainly existed but, overall, most people at all levels considered it to be reasonable and appropriate. Quality of working life was a key theme and this was seen as an extension of the overall push for improved quality of life for everyone in society. Graves' Level 1.6 (care for others) view of the world was gaining in strength. Our red zone view of the world was slowly being impacted by blue zone sensibilities.

In the 1980s things changed. Many of us hadn't noticed the change emerging. Suddenly we were in the midst of a push for 'quality' and 'international best practice' – and a direct implication of this was that profits could be improved and people could make more money. 'Greed is good'[5] had hit and many of the established practices were swept away. The gulf between the 'haves' and the 'have nots' suddenly widened in the Western world and social inequality was more obvious than had been the case for many years. A combination of Graves' Level 1.5 (excel) and Level 1.3 (power) views of the world bit back and again became dominant for many people and this was seen by the fact of money and 'success' increasingly meaning few restrictions on those that had power. For many, the good times had arrived and would continue forever. It took the 'stock market adjustment' of 1987 to shake our confidence but even

---

5   This was the theme popularised in the 1987 movie *Wall Street*.

that did not really register for many until the early 1990s. The red zone was seeking to reassert itself.

We spent the 1990s arguing that the excesses of the 1980s were over. But the red zone genie was back out of the bottle. The combination of Graves' Level 1.5 (excel) and Level 1.3 (power) worldviews was dominating and weaker organisations and individuals were swallowed up: globalisation became the catchword and international investors became the drivers of management philosophy and practice. Then came 2008 and the Global Financial Crisis and, despite the obvious evidence that the dominant approach was sadly lacking, the response was largely to retreat further into the red zone. From observing legislation enacted since then, given the current political and business environment, nothing is really likely to change. Today the reality is largely that 'red zone rules'.

Which begs two questions:

1.   Has the last 100 years brought about any real change?

2.   Does it matter?

First, does it matter whether or not any real change has occurred?

Yes.

Today we have the best educated and most technologically capable macro society in history. We have the ability to do things that were beyond the imagination even of science fiction writers 100 years ago. The rate of acquisition of knowledge is constantly increasing. In just my lifetime the things I have seen include the movement from small propeller driven aircraft to space exploration, the completion of the first stage of the human genome project, and the advancement of medical science to the point where we are able to deal with most major diseases facing mankind. Operating with lesser ability to deal with ambiguity and complexity has been very good to us. It is beyond my comprehension to envisage what learning will occur in the future. It would be a tragedy of major proportions if such technological advancements were not matched by a development in the way we interact with other people.

Second, has the last 100 years brought about any real change?

I believe the answer to this is 'yes ... but'.

The 'yes' part is easy.

There is a significant body of knowledge that demonstrates both the need to treat people with dignity and respect and that demonstrates the benefits available to organisations and society when this is done. Virtually every management course in the world teaches this. Probably every organisation – be it for-profit, not-for-profit, private or public sector – would have little difficulty with the adage that 'our people are our greatest asset'. Those organisations that produce 'values statements' invariably have something about 'caring for people'. In other words, the last 100 years has brought about 'real change' in terms of knowing that people are not really expendable objects that can be bought, sold, used and discarded at the whim of management and owners.

'But' ... and here is the crunch ... some years ago I raised the issue of 'education' and 'learning'.[6] I suggested that 'learning' has not occurred unless the knowledge imparted by education manifests itself in behaviour. We can measure changes in knowledge by some form of assessment such as a test or examination. And we do just that. In my own university teaching in the United States and Australia I, like every other teacher, have set examinations that assess the extent to which a student has acquired knowledge from the course taught. The difficulty lies in knowing how much of the knowledge exhibited in such assessments will actually be transformed into learning. Will it have a behavioural impact on the student?

I suggest that, all too often, we confuse 'education' or 'knowledge' with 'learning'. We assume that because a person knows something they will then demonstrate this knowledge in their behaviour. And the assumption is patently false – at least in part because we fail to take into account the fact that our value systems can change as we respond to events around us as well as to changes in our own mental and emotional states.

From the studies of the last 100 years we 'know' that organisations staffed by highly competent and committed people will outperform those with less competent and/or less committed people. We also 'know' that people who have a reasonable balance between work and personal life perform better, in

---

6   D.G. Long, *Learner Managed Learning: The Key to Lifelong Learning and Development*, 1990, Kogan
     Page, London and St Martins Press, New York.

the long term, than those whose lives are less well balanced. We 'know' that we need sufficient stress for us to perform but not so much stress that we are rendered inefficient or incapable. We 'know' that people are social creatures who need interaction with other people. We 'know' that customers respond well to service and that those organisations whose staffing levels and training are such that customers feel they receive service will outperform those in which 'customer service' is seen as an oxymoron.

We 'know' all these things and much more. The difficulty is that, in the main, we have not 'learned' them. Effectively, in Spiral Dynamics' terms, we have not allowed our internal worldviews to develop to the stage where they can comprehend the full import of what is known and to enable us to implement such knowledge in the most efficacious way possible. We have allowed many of the external demands that surround us to prevent the shift in internal value systems about which we have learned and to which we have given at least intellectual assent.

Over my years of consulting and teaching I have had many discussions with managers, executives and directors about this. Time and again these people say to me words like:

> I am caught in a dilemma. My education has made it clear that we need to have staffing levels that allow people to have balance in their lives and so that we can provide customer service close to the level customers want. But we are driven by the stock price. If we don't return profits that are comparable with or better than those of our competitors and of the market generally, the institutional investors will dump our stock. It is absolutely critical that in the quarterly reports we are able to show that our costs are minimal – and we can only do this by keeping staff levels down to the lowest possible level. I'm sorry, Doug, I can follow the arguments for a different approach regarding people – I just cannot implement it.

In most organisations and for most people, Spiral Dynamics' Level 1.5 (excel) and Level 1.3 (power) worldviews trump Spiral Dynamics' everything else because of the greed that all too often lies behind them. We are in a red zone world.

From my observations, it seems that some 85–90 per cent of managers, executives and directors are caught up in this dilemma. Daily they face a conflict between what their studies have told them will bring long-term results for their organisations and the short-term demands placed upon them by market forces. When their reputations and remuneration are integrally linked with the market performance of their stocks, which way will they jump? There is an old adage that says 'what gets rewarded is what gets done'. If rewards are given for short-term expediency such as reducing staff levels, making existing staff work harder and longer for little or no extra pay, cutting back on customer service (or 'upselling' customers to things that are not really wanted) and the like, then these are the things that will get done. The penalties for failing to do these things are too severe. If you doubt this, simply ask any company chairperson, chief executive officer or other senior executive (whether public or private sector) what has happened to their colleagues or themselves when they failed to deliver what the market or their bosses demanded. The Level 1.5 (excel) and Level 1.3 (power) worldviews of Clare Graves' Spiral Dynamics remain dominant in those who see success primarily as equated with wealth.

Back in the days before 'international best practice' and/or 'globalisation' it was a slightly different scenario. These were the days (in Australia, probably up until the 1980s) in which organisations, in the main, were controlled by local boards and generally the investors were from the home country. Under such a situation the main comparison was with other local organisations. The flow of money from one country to another was, very often, more difficult than today and, with a different cost of living, people were prepared to accept lower returns on money invested. Remuneration of executives was generally lower and more tied to national standards. In many countries, a social obligation was felt and acted upon by organisations that saw themselves as having a dual responsibility – one to their shareholders and another to their community. The negative aspects of Spiral Dynamics' Level 1.5 (excel) worldview were less prominent.

But those days are gone. Today there is widespread interchange of executives from one country to another. Today international investors will move their money from one place to another based on less than a percentage point difference on money invested. Today a product may be produced in one country from components made in a myriad other countries, and, on a daily basis, investors watch the reported and predicted results of the companies involved. Based on this data they will buy and sell without regard for national sensitivities and/or cultures.

So are 'best practice' and 'globalisation' bogies we should fear and seek to avoid? Not necessarily – but we should perhaps exercise some caution. There are many benefits that can accrue to nations, organisations and individuals from these. In many places, best practice and globalisation have resulted in lower prices for a range of goods and services. Most countries have benefited from many of the overseas executives who have come to them while many of their people have been able to make significant contributions overseas. Spiral Dynamics' Level 1.5 (excel) worldview level can be very positive!

Christopher Stephenson, one of my DBA students, drew attention to this in his thesis.[7] Typical of comments made to him during his research were:

> *Are the management team incentivised for strategic thinking? I think not. They're incentivised as everyone's told you by short-term goals. Also, we don't expect to last more than three or four years in the job so what's our incentive? It's not LTI (long-term investment) it's short-term bonuses; short term survival.*

> *Sometimes, you get seriously under pressure and when you are under pressure you get seriously into defence mode and you're making sure that you defend number 1 at the detriment of anything else.*

> *Quite often we [CEOs] know that it's the wrong decision ... [but] we have a set of instructions, we have a set of deliverables, and we know it can't be done ... but it still has to be done – you're told 'just do it!'. I'm told to cut my costs by 20% and I know I can't do it because I'm already lean – the only way to do it is to cut into muscle and that means I won't be able to close deals in 6 months time. The Board knows the impact but the financial release to the market is coming up in a few weeks and that means I have to cut [to meet market expectations]. As a CEO, you're between a rock and a hard place.*

Even the executives themselves admit that its one thing to know what should be done: it's another thing to do it. There is a clash in value systems between what one knows should be done and what one actually does. Even when people know a blue zone approach is needed, they are forced into perpetuating red zone behaviour.

In the commercial field we need to recognise that, short term, the bottom line on a profit and loss account is not necessarily the sine qua non of business. We need to recognise that short-term profits and results may give us long-term business failure with the consequent loss of thousands of jobs and negative impacts on the overall economy.

---

7   C. Stephenson, *What Causes Top Management Teams to Make Poor Strategic Decisions?*, 2012, unpublished thesis for the degree of DBA from Southern Cross University.

Ultimately we need to realise that the research and theory from the past 100 years contains truth that needs to be heeded and implemented. Central to such implementation is that management education is then applied in the workplace. And central to this management education is the truth that people are the most important asset for any country or organisation. And the effective implementation of this is 'blue zone'. Without highly competent and highly committed people both organisations and nations fail. The blue zone is the domain of creativity, collaboration and optimism (see Figure 1.1 on page 14).

The ongoing task facing governments, boards and executives is to recognise this truth in practice as well as in theory and to create environments in which it both can and will be applied. In the short term such recognition might mean lower profits and dividends. In the long term such recognition will mean stronger organisations and a better national and world economy. Unfortunately this change to stronger organisations and a better national and world economy will never happen until our leaders are able to handle the increasing degrees of ambiguity and complexity that are involved – and until people are prepared to modify their behaviour to fit the values that ought to be implemented rather than the ones that are all around them.

But there is application outside of the business or commercial world, too. At least in the Western world we have an increasing incidence of family breakdown; we have increasing marginalisation of the poor and disadvantaged; we have the demonising of certain faiths because of the actions of a fanatical fringe sector; we have animosity towards refugees who flee from violence of war and persecution seeking safety and security for themselves and their families; we have the seemingly intractable problems of the Middle East; we have economic driven piracy in places like the South Atlantic Ocean and the South China Sea and politically driven piracy in the Mediterranean Ocean – and so I could continue. The common factor in all of them is that the worldviews held by leaders – those in authority and with power – are not appropriate for the ambiguity and complexity that now exists throughout the world and with which we are all increasingly confronted. By and large our leaders are dominated by the red zone of fear rather than by the blue zone of courage.

Recognising and applying these truths is a constant challenge to the Gravesian value systems practised by many today. Too many people want everything to fit into their world rather than, in response to emerging conditions, personally changing the way they think. It is far easier to remain in the red zone than it is to shift our brain's locus of control to the blue zone.

Until people are open to developing their worldviews – progressing up the Spiral – and are helped in making such moves, things won't change. Having your brain's locus of control firmly in the blue zone requires a worldview that can deal with large degrees of ambiguity and complexity – and that requires a primary spiral position that is at least at Graves' Level 2.1 (process or integrated systems) – a situation that is far from where the majority of people and the majority of political, business, religious and societal environments are today.

Even a superficial examination of today's world makes it clear that values and a worldview based on the red zone area of brain control is falling far short of where we could be. The tragedy is that either we don't want to make the shift to the blue zone or, hopefully more likely, we don't know how to make the change. So just how do we develop a blue zone locus of brain control and Third Generation Leadership?

8

Developing 3G Leaders and Third Generation Leadership

She was absolutely beautiful. She was slim with long golden-red hair, beautiful brown eyes and an exquisitely chiselled nose. These were the features that first attracted your attention. Everyone who saw her took a second look. It was love at first sight. The hair determined the name: she had to be 'Honey'.

But at two years old her life so far had been far from what she deserved. This gorgeous Belgian Shepherd dog had been beaten with brooms or any other instruments to hand – by the women who 'cared' for her. Her jaw and other bones had been broken and some of her teeth had been knocked out. She had been badly abused. Now she had been rescued by the RSPCA and given short-term shelter by a Belgian Shepherd breeder friend of ours. But long term our friends could not keep her so Honey needed a new home. When first we met, Honey was cowering away from the others and her eyes held a look of apprehension. Winning her trust was never going to be easy: helping her grow into a mature, well-adjusted dog was a task worth taking on but with no guarantees of success.

Honey turned 12 this year. Yes, she has arthritis and now she walks slowly and with a limp – however, she loves her walks and is a wonderful companion who soaks up love and gives love and affection to the family – but, at times, there are still hints of apprehension in her eyes and in her demeanour even though for ten years she has never been struck, shouted at, or experienced any other punitive action. Deep down the experiences of those first two years have caused a scar that even a long time with a loving, caring family cannot fully heal.

Honey is not dissimilar from some people with whom I have worked over the past 40 or so years. Back in the mid 1960s I started helping children and other people with problems. I have vivid memories of a young boy from a dysfunctional family who was given the chance of a life in new surroundings. He then lived in a foster home for some time before starting an apprenticeship. Today he is a successful tradesman who employs others – especially young people who are having problems of their own – and who gets great satisfaction from seeing these people grow and develop. The scars of his early life are still there: but operating from 'the blue zone' has enabled him to put things in perspective – something a person can do but a dog cannot.

There have been many others I have tried to help – not all of them success stories – and there are times when it's easy to despair about the chance of development occurring. But I still see some of these people around and the one thing I find rewarding is that invariably they come up to me and express appreciation for the security, stability and encouragement that was provided – even if it was only for very short periods. Young people who had been thrown out of home or who were in trouble with the law; people who considered themselves unemployable for whom I have provided jobs or have assisted with job hunting; people who have been badly hurt and who will never totally recover from the mental and physical damage they have experienced. In my value set these vulnerable people are prominent among those to whom leaders across the board (not just those in the social welfare sector) should devote time and effort – failure to do so will mean today's societal problems continue unabated.

John Corrigan[1] makes the point that, back in 1819 when the Prussians introduced modern schooling, the bulk of the population (94 per cent) were destined for the 'volkschulen' and the emphasis was on obedience – if you don't do as you are told you will be punished. This was enforced by harsh discipline and rote learning. For the next 5.5 per cent (the 'realschulen') conformance was the main organising principle and this produced the professionals who supported the state (the other 0.5 per cent went to 'academie' which were organised around engagement to allow that elite group to fully develop). Clearly, in this model, there was no need for leaders to place any emphasis on the development of the vast majority of their followers.

I have been talking and writing on the subject of Third Generation Leadership for some years now. One of the questions I frequently encounter is 'how can I develop a Third Generation Leadership approach in myself and how can I bring about a Third Generation Leadership environment for the people

---

1   John Corrigan, *This is the REAL Education Revolution*, 2010, Group 8 Education, Sydney.

with whom I work?'. The answer lies in commitment to change both in oneself and in the environment over which the leader has any form of influence.

I believe true leaders help others to grow. While First and Second Generation Leaders can do this with some people, Third Generation Leaders have the ability to help everyone grow. In order to commence this process, however, those leaders involved need to confront two key questions:

1.   Is your current leadership approach getting you the results that you want right now?

2.   Are you reasonably confident that, by maintaining this approach, you will continue to get the results you want in the future?

If the response to both questions is 'yes' then, no matter the reality in relation to any need for development, the leader involved will not be seriously interested in any change. If the answer to either question is 'no' then the leader involved *may* be interested in making some changes – but equally they may not yet have reached the point where they are psychologically ready to make changes. If the answer to both questions is 'no' then you are probably dealing with a leader who is looking for answers and for whom there is a reasonably high probability that they will consider making changes. With these people it is possible to facilitate change and growth.

So what are the steps to facilitating growth in others? It seems to me that most change processes today are predicated on an assumption that some at least of what currently exists is 'OK'. There seems usually to be an a priori assumption that the status quo has some elements that don't need to change. This was certainly the case in the education field where much of the research for Third Generation Leadership was conducted.[2] Most education reform was based on the premise that the current approach needed tweaking – the result was that the system continually improved but much of what was being done was never going to bring about the results that were needed. John Corrigan challenged this assumption, approached the issue from a totally different perspective, and schools and lives were transformed both in Australia and in England. The same applies in every other field. For Third Generation Leadership to come into being we need a shift in the very foundations on which our current leadership models are based – we need the understanding

---

2   A summary of the research base for Third Generation Leadership is supplied in the Appendix.

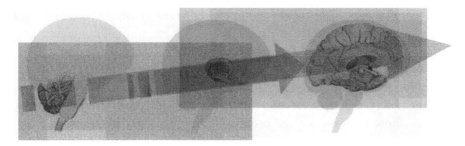

Figure 8.1   The Necessary of Shift in Locus of Control

and application of neuroscience that allows us to transfer our brain's locus of control from the red zone to the blue zone. And that opens a totally new premise and enables a totally new development process to emerge. The key is shifting the brain's locus of control from the red zone to the blue zone. And this is where the issue of brain plasticity (see Chapter 6) becomes so important. The research conducted by John Corrigan, Andrew Mowat and myself makes it very clear that any person can shift their brain's locus of control as they close down inappropriate synapses and open new circuits. We have also ascertained that this is a remarkably simple thing to do and to maintain (see Figure 8.1).

In facilitating this shift, first, recognise that this may take time. There are at least two distinct factors leading to change being desirable. The first factor affecting development is if the person, like our dog Honey, has suffered physical and psychological hurt and damage. While this hurt and damage may have been done in a very short period, repairing that damage may take many years – and may never actually happen despite your best efforts.

The second factor affecting development is if a person is finding that their existing worldview (i.e. combination of levels on Professor Clare Graves' Spiral Dynamics model) is failing to deal with that which is being encountered. If a person has been successful in the past through using their present approach, they may be frustrated and angry that they are not getting desired results today. In this case, again, for them to actually implement any change can take considerable time, no matter how much they may intellectually agree such change is necessary. For many there will be repeated attempts to fit the new world into the old model – which generally leads to increasing frustration, anger and a sense of total futility.

When encountering either of these cases, have high expectations that, at some time, the other will grow and develop – but be prepared to accept disappointment: and be willing to persevere even when the going gets really tough. Until the other person actually realises that conditions have changed or are changing and that they personally need to change nothing will happen. Until the other person understands that, through you as a leader, there are now new emerging conditions that are supportive of them, nothing is likely to happen. From a values perspective that is perfectly 'OK' – as Graves said, allow people to stay where they are if that is what they want. Of course, from that person's desired end results perspective the situation may be quite different – it may in fact be impossible for him or her to actually achieve their desired results until they do make a shift up Graves' Spiral! However, ultimately, only the individual him or herself can be the one who can make any decision to change.

Third, demonstrate absolute and total acceptance of the 'other' as they really are – everyone needs to know that he or she as a person is always totally accepted even if their behaviour isn't appropriate and/or isn't bringing about the results desired. Create a 'safe' zone. Develop the ability to make clear the distinction between 'the person' and 'the behaviour' – and show 'the person' that you genuinely care. You as the facilitator need to demonstrate the emerging, positive conditions – the blue zone – even if such demonstration is repeatedly rejected by the other person.

Fourth, provide a place of total safety where they can feel secure and wanted – away from any form of violence including sarcasm, ridicule and 'being shouted at' or being 'talked down to'. Particularly if you are working with someone who is grappling with the fact that his or her past leadership approach is no longer proving effective, this is critical. From my experience, people in this category are super-sensitive to any hint of criticism regarding how they have been operating and/or how they are trying to operate now. And for a person who is dealing with behavioural issues and who is trying to change behaviours, this place of total safety is especially important when he or she drops back into past behaviour and again acts inappropriately.

Fifth, start from where he or she is now – not from where you would like them to be, and move at his or her pace – not yours. Your respect of the other needs to be total and immediate: earning their respect and trust for yourself is a drawn-out and gradual process.

Sixth, celebrate small successes. When we first met Honey, an initial success was for her to come to us and allow my wife and family to pet her – she was especially terrified of women because of the treatment she had received. Small successes when celebrated and reinforced tend to cascade –

set achievable 'step targets' and concentrate on how far you have come, not on how far you have to go.

Seventh, be authentic. Let the other know when you are happy and/or unhappy with your life in general as well as with the other person. Be a role model that shows how you cope with life's various issues and problems – even if you feel you should cope with them differently. Let the other see that it's 'OK' to fail – that the really important thing is how you deal with 'failure' and disappointment and with life in general.

In my experience, for any such facilitation to be possible a leader needs to shift his or her brain's area of control from the red zone to the blue zone. In other words, for change and development to occur, this brain plasticity needs to be operative in both the leader *and* the follower. Trying to facilitate mental shift from a Second Generation Leadership perspective invariably results in frustration because of the issue of conditional respect. In a Second Generation Leadership worldview there is always the possibility of an underlying fear that the facilitator's expectations are not being met. The writer R.D. Laing[3] put it rather well:

> *I feel you know what I am supposed to know*
>
> *but you can't tell me what it is*
>
> *because you don't know that I don't know what it is.*

In this Second Generation Leadership situation there is a constant temptation for a person to try to give the facilitator what he or she believes the facilitator actually wants rather than focusing on his or her own real development and growth needs. The end result can be a failed facilitation with guilt on the part of the person and disillusionment on the part of the facilitator – both of which will result in regression further into the red zone rather than progression into the blue zone.

In facilitating growth and development, coupled with the facilitation issues is the issue of time – 'cost'. In today's world there is an emphasis on immediacy. Graves' Level 1.5 (excel) level is very dominant! Services are measured by what they cost rather than by what they achieve. People are seen as 'resources' that are capable of being changed when they reach their 'use-by date'. Short-term

---

3   R.D. Laing, *Knots*, 1970, Random House, New York.

expediency trumps long-term investment. Economic rationalism is still king – even if it has been exposed as an emperor without clothes.

Developing Third Generation Leaders is all about helping people develop to the stage where they can deal appropriately with the levels of ambiguity and complexity they encounter and with which they are responsible for dealing. Such development does not happen overnight. Given the 'bottom line' emphasis by most organisations (including governments and social service operations) it is unlikely that most organisations will be prepared to invest the time and money necessary for the new worldview to emerge in the near future. This reluctance is probably exacerbated by the fact that, once Third Generation Leadership is established, the demise of Second Generation Leadership organisations is imminent. Those of us wanting to develop as Third Generation Leaders and to get Third Generation Leadership established can expect opposition.

This issue of opposition to change and a desire to revert to inadequate approaches has been recently highlighted (May 2010). In the United States there appear to be moves in Texas to have the country revert to some form of theocratic emphasis at least in the education textbook arena. Resistance to the new has been illustrated also in Queensland in Australia where there are moves to introduce non-scientific theories (intelligent design) into some science classes, and in the state schools of New South Wales in Australia where attempts to introduce the study of ethics as an alternative to 'Bible in Schools' was vociferously opposed by many of the Churches and Church leadership. Rather than developing personal understanding and leadership about, and growing through, the levels of ambiguity and complexity that ideally should be espoused in education, there appear to be vested interest moves to revert to approaches that provide simplistic answers to some very complex issues. As Lehrer[4] points out in Chapter 7 of his book, when we have 'certainty' we will tend to ignore anything that challenges our view – no matter how verifiable and indisputably accurate the facts of the challenge may be. Which is part of the reason why the pundits are so often wrong!

But what about in other areas?

Quite apart from these education examples, nowhere is this failure to understand and grow through the various levels of ambiguity and complexity more obvious than in the realm of international relationships. There is ample evidence to show that sanctions against countries do not have any impact

---

4   Lehrer, *The Decisive Moment*.

other than further disadvantaging those who are most vulnerable. This was seen in the sanctions against South Africa in the days of apartheid and in the sanctions against Iraq prior to the US-led invasion. It has been seen for years in the sanctions against North Korea. It is increasingly seen in the sanctions against Hamas and the Gaza Strip, and it is seen in the sanctions against Iran. An ideological commitment to failed approaches such as invasion, blockades, sanctions and retaliatory violence is evidence of total failure in political leadership development and an inability to deal with the levels of ambiguity and complexity that exist in today's world.

In the First Generation Leadership world and in the Second Generation Leadership world, we are beset by leaders who seem to operate under the old maxim: 'My mind's made up. Don't confuse me with the facts!'

This has relevance, too, when we consider the appropriateness of leadership development in the business world. In 2009 and 2010 I surveyed 43 organisations operating in Australia as to what they were doing in terms of developing their leaders for tomorrow. Twenty-two of these organisations were operating internationally and, of these, 18 were non-Australian corporations. Four organisations were in the not-for-profit sector and two of these were major, very well known organisations. Only one organisation (a not-for-profit with some 500 employees) said that they did nothing in terms of leadership development and only one organisation (again, as it happens, a not-for-profit but with some 350 employees) was utilising the insights from neuroscience in their leadership development. All the other organisations were certainly aware of the need to ensure a fit between the leadership programmes they used and the culture of their organisation but none was attempting to question the Second Generation Leadership approach that was advocated by the universities and/or consultants they were using. This was, in part, because, for most organisations, there was a low level of real acknowledgement from top management that their culture needed to change. None of these organisations said that they were totally satisfied with the results of their training yet they were not comfortable about questioning the premise from which their suppliers were operating.

Today there is an urgent need for true leaders and good leadership – and good leadership is focused on the future and centred on other people. Good leadership engenders engagement of people with the leader, with each other, and with those things that need to be done in order to achieve desired performance. The leaders we need for the future are those who seek to create a better future for everyone – and that requires that we help everyone grow and develop. Part of this development is in relation to actual skills – competence – but much of it is also in relation to the ability to deal with ambiguity and complexity.

It is this last area that is all too often lacking in many leadership development programmes. While the need for development is fully acknowledged by the traditional providers of leadership development, most such providers appear to have a vested interest in promoting their existing approaches (even if these are totally repackaged). They promote packages that look primarily at developing leadership technical competence rather than approaching the issue from a new platform. The vast majority of them provide little or no input on matters such as the neuroscience contribution to our understanding of leadership and worldviews – the Gravesian material – understanding of which is so critically needed today.

If we are to develop Third Generation Leadership cultures, it is important to first realise that a culture change is needed to develop Third Generation Leaders (3G Leaders).

So the key questions become: 'How do we learn to manage down the red zone and manage up the blue zone?' or 'How do we actually move our brain's locus of control into the blue zone?' or 'How do we become 3G Leaders?' and 'How can we encourage people to develop their ability to deal with increasing ambiguity and complexity?'. The answer appears to lie in two simple, very common, basic aspects of the way in which we communicate.

9

Communication – the Key to Third Generation Leadership

Many years ago I was approached by a manufacturing company that had serious problems in relation to occupational health and safety issues. About 5 per cent of the company's workforce comprised people coming to the country on four-month temporary work visas. This was part of an economic support programme that the country offered to some of its smaller neighbours. These workers were very enthusiastic and they were hard workers. Many of them returned regularly under the economic support scheme.

The company involved took its social responsibility to all workers very seriously. No matter where they came from, no matter whether they were employed on a short-term visitor basis or on a full-time, local citizen basis, there was a comprehensive orientation programme. In addition, when these short-term workers arrived at the factory, whether or not they had previously worked there, they underwent a further one-week paid induction programme that covered all aspects of their jobs as well as information about fitting into the local community. The job induction was very hands-on and concentrated on developing skills and on working safely. Until this training was completed and the necessary level of knowledge and skill could be demonstrated, no worker was allowed to operate any machinery in the factory itself. Despite this training and the very high quality of on-the-job supervision that was provided when they did get to work in the factory, workplace accidents occurred with monotonous regularity and some of them were very serious – workers losing fingers or parts of fingers or, in the incident which led to me being brought in to help, losing a hand.

My initial theory was that there must be some deficiency in the training philosophy and material. This theory was quickly disproved. The material was of an extremely high standard and those people providing the training were very professional and highly skilled both in the work being taught and in their training competence. I started to look elsewhere. What quickly became apparent was that English, the language used in the training and on the factory floor, was not the first language for these short-term employees. It was also apparent that, although all of these workers had a reasonable level of conversational English, they did not have an adequate grasp of technical terms and, coming from basically agrarian economies, the mental shift required to work in a high pressure factory environment was not easily made.

Working in the company legally and on a permanent basis were representatives from all of the countries that were being helped by this economic support package. I recommended that the company use these people to translate the training material and all documentation into the various languages involved. I recommended also that the company use these translators as assistant trainers during the orientation and induction training. This was done. Within days the impact was apparent. The incidence of workplace accidents among these short-term employees plunged to below that of the full-time employees (and that was already at a very low figure). Productivity soared and everyone benefited. Suddenly the people involved found it easy to understand and internalise what they were being taught. The problem lay not in what was being taught. The problem lay in the way the training was communicated.

In the early 1990s three local competing organisations in Sydney were merged in order to provide economies of scale, more efficient services, and in order to deal with new competition. The merger had been approved by the relevant authorities and a new organisation with some 5,000 employees came into being. The first action taken by the new board was to hold a retreat for all directors and the executive team to agree the way forward. At that session, which I facilitated, it was decided that all employees should be told what the company intended to achieve over the next five years and, in broad terms, how this was to be achieved – including the fact that the company would have reduced its workforce by about 1,500 people in the next two years. The chairman[1] stressed that the issue of *what* was to be achieved was not negotiable. Equally, he stressed, the *how* was a matter on which the board wanted widespread discussion and input from every level in the company.

The CEO decided to use an innovative communication process designed to ensure every employee received the same information within the next few weeks. Each executive held a workshop with his direct reports and, at each

---

1   Reference to this company and its communication process is found in Allan Moyes, *Quality Leadership*, 1997, The Centre for Leadership Studies, Australia.

of these meetings, the CEO was present to ensure consistency of message as well as to answer questions that the executive may not have been able to answer. Each of these direct reports (i.e. each senior manager) then repeated the process with his or her direct reports and, at each of these workshops, the appropriate functional executive was present to ensure consistency of message as well as to answer questions that the manager may not have been able to answer. This process was repeated on a cascading basis and, over the period, every employee became involved in the process. Feedback from these workshops was, at every stage, fed upwards and attention was paid to the issues raised.

At the end of the two years, every target had been met while anticipated profitability had been exceeded. The company had done far better financially than had been originally planned. The entire staff reduction process was completed without any industrial disputes and in a way that maintained the commitment of remaining staff as well as ensuring departing employees continued to feel that they had been treated fairly by the company. As Moyes[2] says, 'it was an example in which flow of information produced dramatic results'.

The truth is that a leader is only as good as his or her communication. My research that resulted in *The Challenge of the Diamond* and *Leaders: Diamonds or Cubic Zirconia?*[3] made that very clear. In my eight facets of leadership, we find *'communication'* in seventh place. I point out in that book that effective leaders are good communicators – and that means being a good listener as well as being clear in what and how you say things whether verbally or in writing. Communication also means using a language that your listeners can understand – it's no use speaking English (or any other language) if your listeners can't understand it and there are no good interpreters around! Similarly it's no use using technical language or jargon if your listeners can't understand it.

Communication also means 'keeping your message simple' as well as checking to see that your listeners have heard and understood your message.

Recently an Australian scholar, Colin Rymer,[4] noted in his doctoral dissertation that most leadership researchers and writers seem to take

---

2   Ibid.
3   Ibid.
4   'Leadership in Australia: How Different are We?', 2009, unpublished DBA thesis through Southern Cross University.

'communication' as a given rather than drawing attention to its importance. He was concerned at the low level of attention paid to this critical component.

The work around 'red zone' and 'blue zone' has added a further element to how we communicate – something that moves beyond 'keeping your message simple'. When I wrote *Leaders: Diamonds or Cubic Zirconia?* I did not have the knowledge of neuroscience that I have today. When I wrote that book, I had no in-depth understanding of the work of Clare Graves, and I had no concept of the 'red zone'–'blue zone' dichotomy which is central to the concept of Third Generation Leadership. Because of this, unfortunately, I inadvertently helped perpetuate the traditional approach – an error that this book now seeks to remedy.

During the 1950s I cannot remember much emphasis being made on 'how' people communicated. I'm not sure that 'public relations' even existed as a discipline back then. However, in 1957 we had Vance Packard's *The Hidden Persuaders* and William Sargant's *Battle for the Mind*, and, in 1964 came Marshall McLuhan's *Understanding Media: The Extensions of Man* in which he introduced the phrase 'the medium is the message'. Without commenting on the content of these works, it seems to me that much of the current emphasis on 'how' we communicate rather than 'how *and* what' we communicate can be dated back to works such as these. When today I look at 'leaders' on television, hear them on the radio or read of them in the written press I often find that it is difficult to ascertain what they really believe and what, if any, is the goal they are trying to achieve other than massaging their own egos. This emphasis on 'how' things are presented rather than on 'what' is presented often results in very shallow, populist approaches that are designed for 'sound bites' rather than for edification. People seem to want to keep themselves in forefront of our minds rather than to inform. In Gravesian terms, they are linked into a Level 1.5 (excel) world with a veneer of Level 1.6 (care for others) while relying on Level 1.3 (power) to make sure they get what they want.

Developing into 3G Leaders requires that we learn how to communicate both the 'what' and the 'how'. We become able to do this once we learn how to manage down our red zones and manage up our blue zones.

For a long time there have been very good initiatives for managing down our red zones. One very powerful means of doing this is meditation and/or prayer in its various forms. Most religions and faiths have long recognised this and have helped people become more calm and focused. The ability to quieten our minds and allow time and space for negativity to dissipate is a wonderful one to learn. But this is only one side of the coin. As I have said before, getting rid of what you don't want is not the same as getting what you do want.

When I was a young man, one of the first performance evaluations I received stated that my physical bearing coupled with my mental attitude had an impact on my communications. I was told that my superiors saw me as being 'challenging' and that those for whom I was responsible saw me as being 'intimidating'. The term that summarised these characteristics was 'you have an unfortunate manner'. This, of course, was in an emerging Second Generation Leadership world run, primarily, by First Generation Leadership people. With the help of a sympathetic boss, I managed relatively easily to change my outward approach to my superiors, but it took me quite a long time to learn how to actually become the leader I aspired to be. I could manage down my red zone. I didn't know enough to be able to manage up my blue zone.

The research by John Corrigan and Andrew Mowat in the education sector in Australia and England[5] has shown that managing down the red zone and managing up the blue zone can be done simultaneously. This is neuroplasticity (see Chapter 6) in a form that is immediately available for all of us to use. Our brain is able to change neural connections and effect a significant shift in our thinking and behaviour by learning some different skills. It requires that we learn:

- powerful questioning;

- observational listening;

- optimistic listening.

The use of these three aspects of communication has a very positive impact on those with whom we are interacting:

- powerful questioning shows respect for the other person;

- observational listening shows people that they are being listened to;

- optimistic listening shows belief in the other person.

---

5   Mowat et al., *The Success Zone*. In this book we also provide the requisite tools.

And these three attributes are those which create an environment in which both we and those with whom we interact are able to grow.

So what are these three aspects of communication?

Powerful questions are those questions that trigger the right responses because they:

- focus on the other person and their thinking, not the detail of the issue or problem;

- are clear of any attitudes and beliefs of the questioner;

- are easy to understand;

- provide useful (rather than interesting) answers from the person with whom the discussion is taking place.

Powerful questions are not easy questions to ask because they are not our default way of questioning. In the past society's approach to questioning has generally been so that the questioner can make a decision or a judgement or so that the questioner can resolve the issue or problem being faced.

In a basically hierarchical society predicated on obedience or conformance (a First Generation Leadership world or a Second Generation Leadership world) such approaches were possible (even if often unsuccessful) but that is no longer the case. Now those in authority (at least in most of the Western world) face the very real probability of overt criticism and loss of respect and authority if their decisions or 'solutions' are wrong or inadequate. The rapid decline in popularity of presidents and prime ministers in countries such as the United States, UK and Australia is evidence of this.

Powerful questioning creates a totally different situation for the person to whom feedback is being given. It says to the other person something like: 'I may not have all or even many of the answers, but we can work through this together' or 'I may not be happy with what you have done, but I respect you as a person and therefore I want to work with you in order to resolve this issue'.

In my experience this is the sort of questioning that elicits a totally different response from what is otherwise obtained. This different response can lead to real behaviour change and to significant growth in both parties. It can also lead to the obtaining of innovative and increasingly appropriate answers to otherwise apparently intractable problems and complex issues.

The very act of changing our default approach to questioning is a powerful tool in starting to manage down our red zone while simultaneously managing up the blue zones of both ourselves and those with whom we are interacting. When this shift commences we are on the way to getting 'what we want' rather than simply getting rid of 'what we don't want'.

Observational listening has the purpose of reflecting back to the speaker what you see and hear. This shifts the leader's attention away from his or her own internal processing (e.g. analysis, judgement and assumptions) – i.e. away from the leader's own thinking – to what is actually happening within the other person's brain processes. Accordingly observational listening harnesses power that may otherwise be unlikely to be readily available for problem resolution.

While powerful questioning may be a new skill for many people, observational listening has been around for many years under such guises as reflective listening, non-directive counselling, etc. Those of us who were trained in Rogerian Counselling (based on the work of Carl Rogers)[6] have been using it in counselling situations for many years. It is listening that picks up both verbals and non-verbals then ensures the speaker understands that the full import of what they are saying and feeling is being heard. Of course, in a Second Generation Leadership world we made a clear distinction between using this for counselling situations and any day-to-day management or leadership matters! Third Generation Leadership sees no such distinction when it comes to resolving difficult issues.

It has been suggested that for the majority of people, listening is most often:

- for opportunities to sound intelligent;

- for a chance to say something funny;

- for how I could sound important;

---

6   A good overview of this approach is found in Carl Rogers, *On Becoming a Person*, 1961, Houghton Mifflin Company, Boston.

- to information I want;

- to external distractions – other noise, music etc.;

- for what's going on for the other person;

- for approval;

- to my own thoughts, not listening to the other person at all;

- to be able to understand the problem;

- for how I can benefit;

- for the opportunity to one-up the other person;

- for the details so that I can help solve the problem;

- for how I can undermine the other person's point of view or position;

- for how I can change or end the conversation.

When we consciously shift our default way of listening away from anything in this list and we concentrate on the real message that the speaker is seeking to give, we further reduce our red zone and we further enhance the blue zones of both ourselves and those with whom we are interacting. The building up of 'what we do want' is increasing in pace. Now creativity and innovation can become realities – now we can start looking for Third Generation Leadership resolutions even to those problems and issues that have arisen out of First Generation Leadership and Second Generation Leadership thinking and behaviours.

The 1G Leader of the First Generation Leadership world listens only when he or she chooses and, even then, only for their own benefit as they believe that they must make a decision or form a judgement. The 2G Leader of the Second Generation Leadership world listens so that they can understand the problem in order to solve a problem or resolve an issue. The 3G Leader of the Third Generation Leadership world listens so that he or she can engage the other person with the solution.

Optimistic listening makes it clear to the other person that there are probably a range of possible solutions to every issue and/or problem. For a whole raft of reasons, a solution that might be nominated by the leader may not be the best possible. Therefore engaging with the other party or parties enables better problem solving and decision-making. When this is done properly the relationship between the parties involved moves to a collegial rather than a hierarchical one and all those involved have the opportunity to experience growth. Now everyone involved is engaged with each other *and* with that which needs to be done.

Optimistic listening is simply not possible when the red zone is dominant. The red zone is focused on oneself and tends to be judgemental. My ego is both in play and at risk here. This is the zone that drives 'me' to being the decision-maker or problem solver. The blue zone is focused on the other and tends to be optimistic and supportive. This is the zone that drives 'us' to creativity, innovation and higher level leaning.

The combination of observational listening and optimistic listening enables the leader to engage the other party in developing and implementing any solution. It effectively removes hierarchical imbalance and creates an atmosphere in which multiple viewpoints can be provided and in which both issue/problem analysis and resolution are team based.

The impact this has on others is immense. It is abundantly clear that authentic and strong attention on another and *for them* is the underlying social mechanism that triggers engagement. As all the research shows, when people are engaged both with activities and those people around them, productivity improves in all areas.

Like it or not, we are now living in what is really (even if not recognised) a Third Generation Leadership world. Today's younger people no longer fit the 'obey or conform' mould of First Generation Leadership or Second Generation Leadership. We see this shift in the general response by younger people to authority whether it is in school, work or society at large. 'Gen Y' are not interested in 'toeing the line' and they are prepared to openly rebel if this is demanded of them. While it is true that young people have always included a rebellious element that offended their elders and the powers that be, today the phenomenon is more widespread than ever before. Young people today demand to be engaged in what they are doing and with the people with whom they are doing it – and through such technology and media as mobile telephony, the Internet, and social networking sites such as Twitter and Facebook they have available the means for making such demands on a scale as has never existed before.

Denise is a Gen Y young woman employed by a chain of small boutique jewellery stores found in major shopping centres across Sydney. She loves her work and, over the year or so she has worked there, is consistently one of the top two people in terms of sales figures. However, Denise is criticised because her sales reflect dollar value and margin rather than numbers of items sold – the argument is that if she 'pushes' more then she will sell more items. The company reduces her hours of work and rosters her for days in which there is usually low floor traffic in the centre where she works (she is employed as a casual) because they consider her to be failing on one of their key performance measures – number of items sold. Then, when over a period of one month, Denise's sales figures indicate that she will now rate lowest on the sales revenue scale, she is given a formal reprimand and told that her job is in jeopardy. As Denise said to me, when talking about her now seeking new employment:

> *They disrespect me. I get customers returning to the store and building up relationships with me and with our branch precisely because I work with them to find out what they want and how we can meet their need rather than foisting stuff on them that they don't really want – and my figures show that I'm good at making sales that have a high profit margin. But that's not enough! It's all b.s! If that's how they're going to operate, I'll go elsewhere.*

Denise's organisation hasn't made any move to a management style that engages people. It operates in a Second Generation Leadership framework – and almost certainly, after she leaves (as she surely will), Denise will ensure that her 'friends' on the networking sites she uses are fully aware of the standard of her current management – ultimately the effect on her employer is likely to be far more negative than that which they (and Denise) really want. Perhaps this issue of the standard of management and the culture of the organisation both contributed to the fact of, during 2010, WikiLeaks receiving so much classified information from disaffected employees.

Engaging people requires a 'blue zone' area of brain control from the leader. Such an approach engenders a blue zone approach in the follower, and when a person is operating in this area:

- they contribute creative and innovative ideas;

- they help others develop a shared sense of what is really important;

- they spend time helping others with their personal learning issues;

- they show consistency between espoused values and personal behaviour;

- they seek out challenging opportunities for people to grow, innovate and improve;

- they focus on a better future;

- they are able to communicate complicated ideas clearly;

- they show empathy and concern when dealing with others;

- they experiment with new concepts and procedures;

- they facilitate the building of collaborative approaches;

- they foster positive relationships with the broader community;

- they present others with a positive approach to change;

- they communicate excitement about future possibilities;

- they ensure that those who did the work get the credit;

- they deal with conflict in a positive and creative manner;

- they share information and knowledge widely and appropriately.

Of course, operating in this way then requires that we provide an environment in which this is both accepted and encouraged.

10

Third Generation Leadership Structures

Eric joined a not-for-profit organisation in Sydney as a senior manager within one of its four operating divisions. His previous experience had been with for-profit organisations that ranged in size from relatively small to very large. The organisation Eric was now working for employed about 70 people on a full-time basis plus approximately 100 people on a casual basis. Eric loved the work and found it both professionally and personally very satisfying. During his early months with the organisation Eric developed good relationships with other employees across the divisions and found that by interacting with these people he was able to do his own work better plus he was able to increase the ability of his colleagues to achieve desired results. Eric had been with the organisation for about six months when a new accountant, Michael, joined the company and Michael quickly became part of Eric's informal network.

This company occupied two levels in a multi-storey building with the administrative divisions on one level and the operational levels (to which Eric belonged) on another. Eric would often flit between the two in order to discuss operational issues and get assistance when required. One afternoon he was called into his boss's office. 'What were you doing upstairs?' he was asked. 'Oh', Eric replied, 'I had a question about costing a particular tender on which I'm working and I knew Michael would be able to help me so I went and saw him. As a result I can now get the tender completed and out tonight'.

His boss was almost apoplectic. 'That's not the way we do it around here and you've been here long enough to know that' exclaimed Eric's boss.

> *If you want to get information from Michael, you come to me first. I will then talk with Michael's boss and he will get you the information. That will then be given to me and I will pass it on to you.*

'That's ridiculous', replied Eric, 'it will take far too long. We need to get this tender out by tomorrow and a process like that means unnecessary delays'. Eric was quickly made aware that these lines of communication were non-negotiable and were to be adhered to. He learned, also, that the same message was being given to Michael by the financial controller. Despite loving their work and believing in what the organisation was set up to do, both Eric and Michael left the organisation within the year.

There are certain things that seem to be self-evident. My research that led to the 1998 book *Leaders: Diamonds or Cubic Zirconia?* indicated that knowing yourself and recognising that you do have leadership responsibilities in at least some areas of life is at the very core of any group of leadership essentials. Most leadership development programmes address this issue.

But there is another issue that is less often addressed – and even then, often not very well. This is the issue of 'creating an environment in which everyone can be successful' – the issue of both the macro and micro structures in which leadership occurs. This 'environment' factor was number eight in the leadership factors I introduced in *Leaders* and, of course, both the physical *and the psychological* environment is a critical factor in the overall achievement of desired performance. For Third Generation Leadership to operate, the environment in which leaders operate – and of which they are a key part for others – must be conducive to actually being a 3G Leader.

Some years ago Sir John Harvey-Jones,[1] a well respected company director in the UK, wrote:

> *If a company is successful it is due to the efforts of everyone in it, but if it fails it is because of the failure of the board. If the board fails it is the responsibility of the chairman, notwithstanding the collective responsibility of everyone. Despite this collective responsibility, it is on the chairman's shoulders that the competition and the performance of that supreme directing body depends.*

No one could accuse Sir John Harvey-Jones of being a 'soft' or 'weak' manager. He was renowned for his no-nonsense, bottom-line orientated approach whether as an executive, CEO, board member or chairman. Yet, as the quote shows, Sir John stresses the importance of harnessing the energies of the people in an organisation as being a critical factor if that organisation is to be successful.

---

1   Sir Adrian Cadbury, *The Company Chairman*, 1995, Director Books, UK.

With First Generation Leadership (1G Leaders) and Second Generation Leadership (2G Leaders) this was not so much of an issue. However, with Third Generation Leadership (3G Leaders) it is critical. Sir John, of course, was speaking in a Second Generation Leadership environment where hierarchy was pre-eminent and in which positional power of one or another form was a force to be used in order to bring about conformance to the wishes of those in charge. However, his message is particularly apt for a Third Generation Leadership world. The difference is that now, with Third Generation Leadership, we have available to us the resources to obtain this engagement by everyone without resorting to traditional hierarchy, positional power and a red zone approach.

Most leaders within our organisations today were developed, and have been successful, under a Second Generation Leadership framework. This is true in politics, business, education, religion and society at large. For these leaders it is easier – and more natural – to change policies, introduce new technologies and increase training of staff in order to try and improve organisational outcomes. This is consistent with an approach that is based on Clare Graves' Level 1.3 (family or tribe), Level 1.4 (legalistic or observe the rules), Level 1.5 (excel) and Level 1.6 (care for others) levels of worldviews. But for Gen Y – a generation of people who want to be involved in decision-making as well as in implementing the decisions; a generation who know that virtually all information is readily available from a wide variety of sources providing you search for it; a generation who are prepared to question the traditional power and authority structures; a generation who want to be engaged not only with what they are doing but also with those people they are doing it with – changing policies, introducing new technologies and increasing training is only a partial answer – and one which, it is becoming increasingly clear, they will not accept in the long term. They are openly reacting against anything which has even the hint of a 'command and control' aspect unless they can clearly see that such an approach is appropriate as, for example, might be the case in response to an emergency.

However, the strategy of introducing new technologies and increasing training *can* work if it is combined with a change in mindset (expressed by a change in culture) throughout our organisations. The greatest point of leverage for bringing about commitment to the introduction of new technologies and increasing training is for leaders themselves to model the new behaviours consistent with the new mindset – i.e. operate from the blue zone. Unfortunately the natural tendency for traditional leaders is to act on the system itself and not primarily on themselves and their own behaviours. The result is one where the emphasis from many leaders becomes one of 'do what I say, not what I do!' – and Gen Y quickly sees through and rejects any such hypocrisy and manipulation.

In order to actually 'walk the talk' – to avoid hypocrisy and cant – the structure within which leadership operates must be an appropriate one.

When my children were very young I used to enjoy taking them out for walks. Children, being children, love to run and dance around looking at various things of interest and they are often totally oblivious to potential dangers such as an unrestrained dog, a car emerging from a driveway, or even (when they have their head down or are looking backwards while running forward) of an immovable obstacle such as a telegraph post. My role was to enjoy the walk with them while 'adding value' through being alert to such dangers and helping the children avoid them. A key 'structural' part of my role was to help protect them from themselves!

One of the key researchers of value to 1G Leadership and 2G Leadership in addressing this issue of structure was Elliott Jaques.[2] Jaques made the point that leaders needed to have the skills of greater conceptual ability and a better ability to deal with complex information than did their followers if they were to provide an environment in which others could be successful. Jaques made it very clear that, the more senior you are in any organisation, the more imperative it is that you have the ability to deal with large amounts of ambiguity and complexity.

Jaques' work is absolutely vital for 3G Leadership. However, we need to carefully examine the form of the hierarchy that now emerges. The structure in today's Third Generation Leadership world must be based on something other than simply efficiency of operations and lines of control – the model encountered by Eric in the anecdote with which I started this chapter. If we are to obtain engagement of everyone not only with what they are doing but also with those they are doing it with, we need to provide a structure in which leaders can earn the respect of their followers through the value-added component they provide to the work of others.

Jaques makes the point that work is essential to us but that we need to be able to apply our full potential in order to fully realise ourselves as individuals. Having leaders who have the ability and confidence to create the right environment for applying our full potential is vital – and that requires the

---

2   Elliott Jaques, *Requisite Organisation*, 1998, Cason Hall & Co, USA.

right level of conceptual ability in the leader. Let's look at these conceptual and complex processing skills.

Jaques argues that some people can work effectively without supervision for long periods while others require at least some guidance for periods as short as a few hours upwards. He also makes the point that neither of these is 'good' or 'bad' – they just 'are'. Coupled to this is the ability to deal with information in a serial or parallel manner. Jaques suggests that there are many levels of this ranging from using practical judgement to overcome immediate obstacles (Strata 1 and 2) through to the ability to construct the complex systems that are necessary in, for example, major multinational companies and government organisations right through to entire countries and world issues (Stratum 8).[3]

The rationale behind these strata is that followers need to have confidence in their leaders – and a key part of building that confidence is the knowledge that the leader can add real value because of his or her advanced conceptual ability. If you like, the leader can see further out or see a bigger picture than those reporting to him or her (like me when I was taking the children for a walk). Jaques suggests that, regardless of any formalised organisational hierarchy that may exist, there is a natural hierarchy that develops based on this conceptual ability. It is clear that the informal structure develops because people trust and respect those who are able to be of help no matter where in the organisational structure they may be located. If I find someone who can add value, then I will tend to trust and follow that person. That is clearly what lay behind Eric's networking in the not-for-profit organisation mentioned earlier.

Jaques[4] developed the concept of 'time span of capacity'. He ascertained

> *that for maximum benefit to an organisation, people at different levels or 'strata' should have the ability to deal with different levels of conceptual and practical complexity.*

In his model, Jaques argues that people at Stratum 1 are able to deal with the complexity and ambiguity involved for about a three-month period; that people

---

3   While not discussing Jaques' work, Thomas P.M. Barnett in his book *Great Powers: America and the World After Bush*, 2009, Putnam, USA, provides an interesting commentary on the positive versus negative impacts of a range of US presidents and their ability to deal effectively with complexity and ambiguity in his discussion of the United States' role in the world.

4   Elliott Jaques, *Time Span Handbook*, 1964, Heinemann, London. See also Elliott Jaques and Stephen D. Clement, *Executive Leadership: A Practical Guide to Managing*, 1991, Basil Blackwell, Inc., Cambridge, MA.

at Stratum 5 are able to deal with the complexity and ambiguity involved for about a 10-year period; while people at Stratum 8 are able to deal with the complexity and ambiguity involved for extremely long time frames.

When we apply this concept in Third Generation Leadership organisations, the new structure (whether for organisations or for society at large) should be one where position in the hierarchy is determined solely by a person's ability to deal with the level of complexity confronting that position – and a red zone culture won't allow this. The fact that we are not doing this in a Second Generation Leadership world is made very clear when we consider matters such as education, road, rail, transport and health infrastructure in many (and probably in most) countries. Most major cities and developed societies are experiencing problems such as serious traffic congestion and health service crises because the infrastructure has not kept up with, let alone ahead of, population growth and other demands.

In May 2010 the *McKinsey Quarterly*[5] headlined an article 'Putting Complexity in its Place' which added another aspect to this issue of complexity. They raised the issue of the 'type' of complexity with which executives have to deal and pointed out that many executives don't really know what types of complexity actually exist for the people in their organisations. They were at pains to point out that some types of complexity were bad for business but other types were actually positive – the important thing is to know the types of complexity with which you are dealing.

It seems that, in some quarters, 'complexity' has become a dirty word. In discussions with friends and colleagues it is not uncommon to hear them talking about the difficulty executives, parents and other leaders have with complexity. One colleague told me of having a client bemoan the fact that 'everything's just so complex these days. Why can't it all go back to being simple?'.

The fact is that today's world is complex. There is no simple answer to the problem of terrorism – despite the political rhetoric that it must be stamped out in this country or that country in order to rid the world of this scourge and the declaration of a 'war' in order to do this. There is no simple answer to any of the problems in the Middle East – despite building a wall to separate Israel from the Palestinian Territories and blockading Gaza or placing sanctions on Iran and all of the other initiatives being taken across the Middle East in order to achieve goals set by various (mainly) outside parties. There is no simple answer

---

5   Online edition.

The Blue Zone
- Affiliation, generosity, goodwill
- Reflective/options considered
- Adaptive decision making
- Imaginative/creative
- Higher order learning
- Slow/resource intensive
- Manages impulsive desires
- Not 'fully functional' until adulthood
- **Seat of optimism**

The Red Zone
- Focused on self
- Sensitive to threat
- Engages 'fight/flight'
- Resistant to change
- Low order learning only
- Fast/efficient/instinctive
- Engages impulsive desires
- Anger/fear/depression
- Highly developed at birth
- **Seat of pessimism**

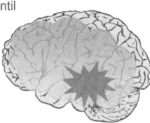

Figure 10.1   Characteristics of Blue Zone–Red Zone

to the problem of national debt and the obvious inability of most countries to be able to rein in their deficits. There is no simple answer to the problem of a reliance on fossil fuels or a push to further develop nuclear energy for peaceful purposes. There is no simple answer to endemic poverty and the gulf that exists between rich and poor – whether of individuals, nations or societies. There is no simple answer to burgeoning health costs, transport and infrastructure costs, or any other of the myriad issues that face individuals, nations and the entire world every day. Those who argue for simple solutions are deluding themselves and those to whom they speak. As the American journalist, H.L. Mencken, is reported to have said: 'There is always an easy solution to every human problem – neat, plausible, and wrong'.[6]

The red zone will always tempt us to take the easy solution because it is resistant to real change. The blue zone, however, will encourage higher level learning to occur and hence is more likely to find a better answer (see Figure 10.1).

What we need is, as Jaques argues, leaders who have the ability to deal with the full gamut of complexity that is encountered. That we don't have this is emphasised by the previously mentioned *McKinsey* article. Complexity such as the number of countries in which an organisation is operating or the variety and numbers of brands and/or people managed are relatively easy to recognise and

---

6   H.L. Mencken, 'The Divine Afflatus', *New York Evening Mail*, 16 November 1917.

to deal with. However, the complexity with which the organisation's people actually deal may be far more related to the actual processes, role definitions and accountabilities that exist in their day-to-day responsibilities. This is why the Leadership for Performance model I introduced in Chapter 2 is so critical. When the leader is actually creating an environment in which his or her people can be successful, both the macro and the micro aspects of complexity are confronted and dealt with. Failure to do this can be very expensive![7]

Without the ability to deal with the entire gamut of complexity commensurate with their level of responsibility, no leader or leadership group operating from the worldview of First Generation Leadership or Second Generation Leadership can actually provide the full value added that they ought to be able to provide for their followers. Today's problems scream this message to all who have ears to hear.

The purpose of structure as nominated by Jaques is to ensure that people at any level are able to provide a clear 'value-added' component to what is done by others. Through this they create an environment in which others can be successful. Had this been the case in the past, many of today's problems would not exist for organisations, internationally, and for life in general. It is only by providing this value-added component that leaders are able to earn the respect of their followers. As the organisation in which both Eric and Michael worked soon discovered, when leaders fail to provide a clear value-added component and lose the respect of their reports, the loss of good employees is a high probability.

An approach to structure that utilises this understanding of value-added and respect is a clear and monumental change from that which pertained under First Generation Leadership and Second Generation Leadership. In both the First Generation Leadership and the Second Generation Leadership worlds, leaders had the expectation that they would be respected (even if often 'respect' was confused with 'fear') and they saw little or no need to respect their followers unless they conformed to the leader's requirements. In these First Generation Leadership and Second Generation Leadership worlds a person could be promoted because of age, length of service, qualifications, etc. secure in the knowledge that, even if they made serious mistakes, they would still be obeyed and hence, in their eyes, 'respected'. A Level 1.3 (power), Level 1.4

---

7   See www.mckinseyquarterly.com/Organization/Strategic_Organization/Putting_organizational
     _complexity_in_its_place_2580

(legalistic or observe the rules) and Level 1.5 (excel) profile of the Gravesian model (Chapter 7) could suffice.

In a First Generation Leadership world – red zone – with 1G Leadership, conceptual ability was not so critical. In a world where everyone 'knew their place' and in which obedience was key, independent thinking was largely discouraged as the manager would make the decisions and closely control who, what, when, where and how work was done.

In a Second Generation Leadership world – red zone with overlays of blue zone – with 2G Leadership, most leadership approaches and programmes are very good at the lower levels of complexity. They deal with the relationship between the leader and the individuals and/or teams with whom he or she interacts. This is important and necessary. Unfortunately it is only part of the story. You can be an effective First Generation Leader or Second Generation Leader with a Level 1.3 (power), Level 1.4 (legalistic or observe the rules), Level 1.5 (excel) and Level 1.6 (care for others) Gravesian worldview and operating in a Second Generation Leadership world.

But the situation is totally different in a Third Generation Leadership world – blue zone locus of control is required. A Third Generation Leadership world requires that the leader treat the follower with unconditional respect secure in the knowledge that, eventually, the leader may earn the respect of their followers. And earning respect is very hard to do unless it is clear that you can add value to that which is done by others. Of course, again it must be stressed that people who are able to operate at high strata levels may not necessarily be operating from the brain's blue locus of brain control – however, a person with their brain's locus of control firmly in the blue zone *and* having the capability to operate at a high stratum level would be a phenomenal leader in any place and especially on the international scene!

During my military service, the Second Generation Leadership world and 2G Leadership was only just emerging. At that time New Zealand was not in any armed conflict – the Emergency in Malaya was over and there was, initially, no involvement in Vietnam. A common message (one that I understand was almost always told to new officers) was: 'Always remember that, when it comes to the crunch, it's not what you wear on your shoulders that's important – it's what holds that up there'. (As an aside, our Army Officers at that time always wore their rank markings on their shoulders.) The message was clear – if you have not earned the respect of others you may have difficulty achieving desired results.

This is where the message of Jaques becomes so important. One of the key ways of earning respect is being able to help people look at bigger pictures and to consider wider implications relating to their decisions and actions. It is the ability to add value to the work of others – and that is a vastly different situation from simply checking other people's work. This is as important today as it was almost 50 years ago.

But true 3G Leadership – the leadership for a Third Generation Leadership world – requires another element – it requires the ability to manage down those areas of the brain that are not helpful in leader–follower interactions while simultaneously managing up those areas of the brain that are helpful – 'Red Zone' (not helpful) and 'Blue Zone' (helpful). 3G Leadership requires that you work on yourself as well as on the system.

Neither 'red zone' nor 'blue zone' is good or bad. Our brain is a unity and we need access to all its areas in order to be fully effective. In fact, as neuroscience has made clear, our neocortical (or blue) zones are not fully operational until sometime in our twenties – until then we all tend to be red zone controlled as evidenced in the 'I am invincible' approach seen in most young people and which leads to most of the reckless behaviour that the majority of us have engaged in at some time in our youth. (And out of which some of us never grow!)

Third Generation Leadership – the 3G Leader – is blue zone dominated.

It is style and substance. It is form and content. Third Generation Leadership involves accepting the past, living in the present, and focusing on the future in such a way that there is a stability and security. Third Generation Leadership makes it clear that, despite anything and everything that happens, there can be hope and confidence not only for oneself but also for those with whom we interact. Third Generation Leadership has the ability to deal with high levels of ambiguity and complexity. Third Generation Leadership provides true value-added to that which is done by others.

Structures that are based on these principles will bear little resemblance to the structures we see today. In today's Second Generation Leadership approach we embrace structural issues:

- Assuming that what we are doing already is pretty close to what is required and that applying new trendy words to existing practices would do the trick.

- Delegating the job to a department or staff group.

- Setting objectives for everything, trying to quantify everything, putting 'quality' or 'customer' into everyone's job goals.

- Making sure that compliance to existing rules and procedures is enforced by middle managers and financial controls.

- Making cost reduction the central issue.

- Putting up lots of posters and distributing flyers and silly slogans guaranteed to raise the cynicism of junior staff. This includes turning the organisation chart upside down to show everyone that the people at the coalface are 'at the top' and that management is a supporting role.

- Making it clear by actions even if not in words that management's role is to authorise and to monitor the change process at lower levels, not to change themselves.

- Reserving detailed training and education for the lower ranks while providing 'executive summaries' for the top echelons.

- Talking about the importance of teamwork while implementing systems of objectives, pay and incentives based upon individual performance.

- Telling everyone we have to 'change the culture' without any real clue as to from what or to what.

- Distributing high-sounding statements of vision and values which do not match the realities of day-to-day life.

- Not listening to those who know that culture change takes time – three to five years is pretty much the minimum realistic time frame – and insisting that 'we don't have that long'.

- When people voice genuine concerns, telling them they should get on board or get out.

- Changing the titles to words like 'leader' or 'facilitator' while keeping the jobs the same and maintaining the same authority structure.

Common to all of these Second Generation Leadership approaches is a deep-seated affirmation and belief that, no matter what we may have said, there is really not all that much wrong with the management system (us) and that the real challenge is to change the behaviour of the people being managed (them). It's a little like *The Emperor's New Clothes* story by Hans Christian Anderson – there was little or nothing there but, until the little boy's shout of disbelief, everyone was prepared to go along with the hoax.

Gen Y (those born since about 1980), living in the Third Generation Leadership environment will not tolerate such deception.

Third Generation Leadership results in a different approach across the entire organisation and, from this, it brings about a significantly different organisation structure, marketing approach and means of assessing performance. In the Third Generation Leadership world the traditional lines of power and authority, together with the traditional distinction and exercise of management and leadership behaviours, are no longer appropriate.

It follows that, if traditional structures are obsolete in the Third Generation Leadership world, new approaches to leadership and management are also required – perhaps even that the distinction between the two is erased. The traditional and established leadership models are totally past their 'use-by' date: a rigid, power and/or authority based approach to leadership is totally inappropriate and using any of these will alienate Gen Y and others who want to be part of a Third Generation Leadership world. Making the changes necessary for a Third Generation Leadership world requires creativity.

In my office hangs a sign which reads: 'Insanity is doing the same thing and expecting different results'. Yet that is precisely what many people and organisations are doing today. Because they are trying to use a red zone/blue zone combination while they operate in a red zone world they stick with the approaches used in the past and wonder why the results obtained are basically the same as before – often quite different from those desired.

The blue zone of Third Generation Leadership is the key. Some years ago there was a warning on many computer input forms: do not bend, fold, spike or mutilate. Today the same warning has also been broadcast by most individuals. People are different. People want to be treated as individuals in their own right.

Today as never before young people tend to be able to move from employer to employer until they find the environment they want – particularly those working in the new knowledge based economy. Accordingly these people will reject approaches which are based on stylised formats which assume a commonality among followers. Gen Y seeks leadership and management practices and processes which recognise the uniqueness of each person. And this requires a dramatically different mindset and philosophy by leaders and managers throughout every organisation.

As Don Beck and Chris Cowan[8] used to say when they taught people about the work of Clare Graves:

- A person has the right to be who he or she is.

- Teach people how to work better, given who they are. Lead them to quality and productivity and decency without trying to or expecting to change who they are. People should not have to change to get your work done.

- Instead build systems that integrate the people, the leadership and the technologies. Facilitate change for those who choose it and grant others the right to be who they are.

This is Third Generation Leadership and the organisations that develop such structures will be tomorrow's success stories.

I once heard a speaker say words to the effect that 'the very things that have made me successful to date are the same things that will stop me being successful in the future'. His emphasis was that the world changes and the new environment requires new behaviours if success is to be maintained.

Just imagine what this would mean in practical terms. We would have organisations that genuinely sought to develop their people. We would have organisations in which honesty prevailed in industrial and employee relations. We would avoid much of the politicking, point-scoring, game-playing and

---

8   Beck and Cowan, *Spiral Dynamics.*

factional fighting that exists today. If applied in the political realm, we would have government and opposition working for the good of the country rather than for their own political agendas. Who knows, we might even find that the Israeli–Palestinian issues of the Middle East, the international concerns about Iran and North Korea, the problems in Iraq, Afghanistan, Africa and all other places that currently exist and will exist are capable of resolution both now and in the future. Perhaps another consequence might be that WikiLeaks and similar organisations will find that there is no need for their work! Now there's a thought!

11

Third Generation Leadership and Accountability

'But, in a Third Generation Leadership world, who's in charge?' That was the question raised by one of the people in a Third Generation Leadership workshop I conducted. 'After all, the role of a CEO is to run an efficient organisation that provides optimal returns to shareholders. If we are to move away from hierarchy and power, how can a CEO (or indeed any executive or manager) actually do what they are supposed to do? How do we hold people accountable?' It's a very good question and one that needs to be answered.

In 2008 one authority[1] stated 'your most important task as a leader is to *make your company more valuable*'. This is impossible without accountability throughout any commercial organisation. It must be noted, however, that the same principle applies in any organisation – even the family. The leader's role is to add value. Remember the performance model I introduced in Chapter 2? (see Figure 2.5 on page 31).

The bottom line in any organisation (including families) is performance. And performance demands accountability. The issue as we move from First Generation Leadership or Second Generation Leadership approaches to a Third Generation Leadership approach is not one of being accountable versus being unaccountable. It is about 'how' and 'to whom' people are accountable.

In the First Generation Leadership and Second Generation Leadership worlds accountability is very clear. Instructions and goals come down the hierarchy and accountability goes back up the hierarchy. This is true whether we are talking about a commercial organisation or any other form of organisation – although in some organisations the hierarchy is not as clear-cut as in the

---

1   Orit Gadiesh and Hugh MacArthur, *Lessons from Private Equity Any Company Can Use*, 2008, Bain & Company, Inc., Harvard Business Press, USA.

commercial world. In a Third Generation Leadership world the issue relates to differences in how this accountability occurs when the traditional power and authority inherent in a hierarchical organisation no longer exists.

Many years ago Peters and Waterman[2] spoke of 'simultaneous loose-tight properties' as a mark of excellent companies. They described these properties as 'fostering a climate where there is dedication to the central values of the company combined with tolerance for all employees who accept those values'.

While there has been considerable discussion (most emphatically, not all of it positive!) about 'In Search of Excellence', and it is certainly indisputable that, subsequent to the book's publication, many of the companies extolled as 'excellent' could no longer be so described, this principle of simultaneous loose-tight properties is central to Third Generation Leadership accountability – although the way in which the properties are utilised may be quite different from that propounded by Peters and Waterman.

One of the reasons a person joins any organisation is because he or she believes that there is compatibility between his or her personal values and the values espoused by the organisation. For example, consider two people with the same qualifications and similar levels of experience. If the personal value set of one person is linked to wealth and power being key ingredients of success, he or she will join an organisation in which the attaining of wealth and power has a reasonable chance of being a reality. If, however, the personal value set of the other person is more orientated to helping those in need, then that person may be perfectly happy to receive lower remuneration for the same sort of duties while working for a charity or other not-for-profit organisation. It may well be that neither person has consciously thought about this compatibility of value sets, but such compatibility will certainly impact significantly on whether or not the person is happy in and remains with the organisation he or she chooses to join. Of course, neither value set is right or wrong – they are simply different – but an individual's value set certainly impacts on that person's expectations and on their performance.

This is why, in Peters and Waterman's work, they emphasised the need for an organisation to have clearly espoused and practised values. Peters and Waterman argue that where there is compatibility between organisation

2   Tom Peters and Robert H. Waterman Jr, *In Search of Excellence: Lessons from America's Best-Run Companies*, 1984, Warner Books, USA.

values and employees' values then the performance of employees has a high probability of being consistent with what the organisation wants and needs. When this is the case, reasonable degrees of flexibility can be allowed in how these people are managed.

But a commonly held view is that values are unchangeable. Read many of the available works and it would appear that some particular value set is deemed to be both universal and immutable. This is understandable for accountability in a First Generation Leadership or Second Generation Leadership world, but it is not the case in a Third Generation Leadership world. In a Third Generation Leadership world, values change.

To understand Third Generation Leadership accountability we need to return to the concepts developed by Clare Graves (Chapter 7) and Elliott Jaques (Chapter 10). There appears to be some consensus that values are emotionally loaded attitudes or beliefs. Accordingly, if I hold a worldview in which 'family' or 'tribe' (Graves' Level 1.2) is what matters most to me, then all of my actions will be centred on doing what is best for, or what best furthers the interests of, the group that I consider to be my family or tribe. Similarly if my worldview centres on hierarchy, control and 'one best way' (Graves' Levels 1.3 and 1.4) or on optimising returns or profits (Graves' Level 1.5) then I will be perfectly happy as part of an organisation that has these values at its core. This is why, in Peters and Waterman's work, they could argue for simultaneous loose-tight properties being the summary of the set of principles they espoused for excellent companies in a Second Generation Leadership world.

It is our worldviews, of course, on which our current approaches to accountability are based. And it is because our thinking is currently locked into this Graves' levels 1.3 (power), 1.4 (legalistic or observe the rules), 1.5 (excel) approach that it is so difficult for us to understand that there may be a different, perhaps even a better, way of ensuring accountability.

The difficulty relating to accountability arises when value sets change – and value sets certainly do change as one's worldview develops through the Gravesian cycle. If a leader's worldview moves to Graves' second tier and the leader moves to a Third Generation Leadership (blue zone of their brain's locus of control) approach, how can a CEO (or indeed any executive or manager) actually do what they are supposed to do? How can he or she hold people accountable for how and what they do towards the achievement of results when we move away from traditional hierarchical approaches to power and authority?

Quite often in my consulting work, I get asked about structural issues. My response from an organisational consulting perspective is identical to the one I use when mentoring individual executives: 'your structure should reflect value added at each level. Tell me, please, what do you do that adds value to the work of those people who report to you?'.

I have found that this question quickly sorts out those who actually provide no 'value added'. It is not uncommon to find that a 'leader' is primarily doing some form of checking the work of their followers in order to provide 'accountability'.

Central to the concept of accountability in a Third Generation Leadership world is that decision-making should be made at the lowest possible level. In other words, those closest to any issue should have the authority to make decisions relating to the issue.

This was the situation that pertained in one of the organisations I referred to earlier. In Chapter 5 I referred to an organisation where employees at all levels had the authority to adjust their work situations in order to deal with personal and other pressing issues. Even on the factory floor they could organise replacements from among their work mates in order to ensure that output wasn't impeded because of a person needing to attend to some urgent personal matter. In this organisation of some 2,500 people and operating over five locations, every person considered him or herself totally accountable for their own actions. Each person, no matter where they were in the organisational structure, also took shared accountability for the quality and quantity of output. The result was high volumes of product, extremely high quality of product, very low levels of industrial accidents (a great occupational health and safety record), and very good returns for shareholders. Effectively the organisation showed trust in its employees and had decentralised much of its decision-making. In this organisation all management levels added value through providing additional information that decision-makers needed in order to ensure that the company was not adversely affected by any employee decisions. Although management could veto employee decisions, such action was extremely rare. The level of trust that had been engendered meant that employees willingly discussed situations with their leaders and accepted advice, but, in these personal problem situations, almost without exception it was the employees themselves who actually made the decisions. The situation in this company only deteriorated (and it did that very rapidly) when a change in chairman brought about rigid controls and effectively centralised decision-making – the company reverted to a traditional approach with largely centralised control.

Because Third Generation Leadership is based on a 'let us' or 'how can we?' premise, as much information as possible is shared. Part of this sharing of information includes ensuring everyone knows the areas in which they can make decisions. People are then encouraged to make decisions in these areas and they are fully informed as to the parameters within which they can make decisions. Because Third Generation Leadership is centred on the brain's blue zone locus of control, such decision-making at low levels of an organisation is not viewed as a threat – rather it is seen as a means of helping facilitate growth in time span of capacity (Jaques) as well as facilitating progression through the Gravesian cycle. In this environment, when mistakes are made (and they are) such mistakes are seen as opportunities for learning rather than being something that warrants punishment or sanction of some kind. In this Third Generation Leadership world, the only real mistake is failing to acknowledge that a decision was wrong or less than optimal and that help or remedial action is required.

Only a leadership worldview that is at Graves' second tier coupled with a structure that is based on Jaques' concept of time span of control and utilised by a leader with his or her brain's locus of control firmly in the blue zone is able to provide this environment and to create these conditions.

As I have said before (Chapter 2) the reality is that most people in virtually every organisation (including a family unit) *want* to do a good job. People want to provide the best performance possible. The problem is that it is the organisation itself that usually prevents them from demonstrating the competence and confidence, the ability and the willingness or readiness, which is central to performance.

I was consulting to a major bank during and just after the major recession of the early 1990s. The project on which I was working had taken some months and, over this time, I had learned that the CEO's motto could well be summarised in the old quote 'be reasonable, do it my way'. This bank had survived the worst of the recession in far better shape than had its competitors and, once economic growth resumed, I asked the chief executive what he would now do differently in order to have the bank move forward. 'Add another layer of supervision', he told me. 'We have come through this remarkably well. We need to make sure that we have all the controls, the checks and the balances, to ensure that we continue on the same path'. I suggested that there may be a different approach possible and quickly found that I was no longer consulting to that bank!

Within a few years this bank was no longer leader of the pack and it wasn't simply financial deregulation that was to blame. Why should a person take personal responsibility for any decisions when he or she knows that someone else is going to go over exactly the same information then give a 'pass' or a 'fail' mark depending on what this supervisory checking level deems should have been done? When an employee's main concern is to second-guess 'the boss' decisions take longer and client service is likely to suffer. In a deregulated financial environment, when a bank client cannot get timely decisions relating to financial issues from their existing bank the client will quickly look elsewhere. There are sound commercial reasons for encouraging decision-making at the lowest possible level of an organisation.

Knowing these sound commercial reasons, most leaders operating from a First Generation Leadership and Second Generation Leadership worldview are somewhat ambivalent about this concept of decision-making being made at the lowest possible level. On the one hand leaders know that it encourages individual responsibility and enables better quality customer service. But on the other hand it is seen as a threat to the control structure and leaders know it is capable of abuse. This is a matter of especial concern in public sector organisations where the use of taxpayer funds is involved or in not-for-profit organisations where community or donated funds are involved. Invariably, particularly if they have had a bad experience because of some abuse of trust, there is therefore a tendency to err on the side of control rather than empowerment no matter what the rhetoric may be. The result is that many organisations fluctuate between centralised and decentralised approaches depending on which is 'flavour of the day' as propounded by some consultancy.

Leaders operating from a Third Generation Leadership approach don't have this ambivalence. They know that there are some things that can be done in order to foster full accountability in an organisation where traditional hierarchical power and authority are not paramount. They know that they can provide appropriate accountability approaches for everyone. Amongst the possible actions to ensure accountability used in Third Generation Leadership are:

- Make it very clear that individual accountability is to be the norm and that this accountability is to oneself, one's peers, one's leaders *and* one's organisation in order to ensure desired results are attained.

- Have a very clear set of organisation values that illustrate the importance of seeing and understanding the interacting variables that form any and all organisations. (These values need to be expressed in behavioural terms.)

- Ensure there is no disconnect between espoused values and practiced values at senior levels – widespread cognitive dissonance will quickly destroy the veneer that seeks to cover any disconnect.

- Use this value set to provide guidelines for everyone on how to deal with the ambiguity and complexity with which every organisation and every individual is faced on an increasingly frequent basis.

- Structure the organisation so that leaders at every level obviously and willingly provide a significant 'value-added' component to that which is done by their followers.

- Remove any grossly excessive status symbols that are dependent upon one's position in the hierarchy and which make it clear who are 'us' as opposed to those who are 'them'.

- Develop a 'no blame' culture in which mistakes are used to facilitate learning and growth instead of being a reason for punishment – if people believe they will suffer penalties for making wrong decisions then they will avoid making decisions.

- Develop a cognitive coaching culture in which everyone is encouraged to shift and to maintain their brain's locus of control in the blue zone.

- Be very clear about organisational goals and the role each person has in achieving these goals.

- Demonstrate trust by ensuring every person in the organisation knows what the organisation is seeking to achieve and, in broad terms, how the organisation intends to achieve these. Be honest and to everyone 'tell the truth, the whole truth, and nothing but the truth'.

- Ensure everyone clearly understands what are 'givens' (i.e. those things that are not open to debate or question) and those things about which there is flexibility.

- For those things for which there can be flexibility, provide very clear parameters within which each person is authorised to make decisions and empower and encourage them to make these decisions.

- Encourage open discussion, questioning and contributions relating to what the organisation is doing and how things could be done better. As most consultants know the people closest to any issue or problems invariably know how the issue could be fixed – their frustration is that, other than the consultant, most people won't listen to them or take their suggestions seriously.

- Encourage people to develop interdepartmental networks and to interact informally to resolve issues and to explore possible solutions to the problems and issues being faced.

Of course, as with the previous chapter's anecdote about Eric and Michael, not everyone will be comfortable with this sort of accountability. Some people are scared of ambiguity and complexity. I have commented already on the fact that ambiguity and complexity bring about different responses (and I will comment on this further in Chapter 12). For some people ambiguity and complexity means an opportunity to grow and develop. For others, this same ambiguity and complexity creates fear and brings about a retreat to a position where clear answers are required – even if such answers either fail to really deal with the situation or deal with it in the short term while creating further problems for the future.

As Andrew Mowat made clear in his comparison between First Generation Leadership, Second Generation Leadership and Third Generation Leadership (see the table in Chapter 6), only a Third Generation Leadership approach – a 3G Leader – has the mindset to be able to effectively lead both those who are able to live with Third Generation Leadership accountability *and* with those who find themselves unable or unwilling to move beyond First Generation Leadership and/or Second Generation Leadership accountability.

Clare Graves (Chapter 7) made it clear that as a person develops their worldview up the cycle, they always retain the ability to utilise earlier worldviews. He makes it clear also that when a person develops to the second tier of the cycle, that person has developed the ability to see everything as an integrated system. At this stage, people find they have the ability to use any of the earlier worldviews in the most appropriate manner. Accordingly the Third Generation Leader is able to adapt his or her leadership approach so that it meets the needs of the followers. By doing this the Third Generation Leader can provide an environment in which the follower has the opportunity to change if they want to while simultaneously allowing the follower to remain with their existing worldview if that is what they prefer. In either case accountability exists.

When people operate in a structure that enables them to be successful (however they may define success) and when a person is comfortable with their form of responsibility and accountability, we have the scene set for self-confident people to prevail. And self-confident people fully understand and accept accountability.

In the early research and experimental stages of developing the Third Generation Leadership concept a variety of commercial organisations tried various aspects of the approach. These organisations were in the highly competitive markets of Hong Kong and Australia and encompassed service, construction, building products, professional services and manufacturing. Without exception, every organisation found that it was possible to sell goods and services at figures significantly above the charges made by their competitors while simultaneously increasing market share and customer loyalty. The application of Third Generation Leadership principles moved transactions away from a cost emphasis to a real value emphasis and the organisations flourished.

This all came together in 2010, when an internationally operating bank tried out a Third Generation Leadership application for 10 weeks and assessed the impact.[3] The bank was totally in control of the assessment. They decided try it out in one of their worst performing areas. By the bank's own assessment, at the end of the 10 weeks:

1.   Team 1 had an increase in the Gross Value of transactions of $47,270,000 which generated $1,645,000 in revenue to the bank.

3   Unpublished DBA thesis by Ian F. Freeman, 'Synergy in SME Financing', Southern Cross University, 2011.

2.   Team 2 had an increase in the Gross Value of transactions of $60,010,000 which generated $1,833,000 in revenue to the bank.

3.   Team 3 had an increase in the Gross Value of transactions of $99,800,000 which generated $3,931,000 in revenue to the bank.

In all, the combined force of three teams over the 10-week trial period generated the following results:

The total value of new Gross Transactions was:	$207,080,000
The total new revenue to the bank was:	$7,409,000
New revenue annualised over was:	$29,636,000

At the end of 10 weeks of operation, the trial programme increased the value of new revenue by a figure of 98.79 per cent. This figure also indicated exponential growth was potentially available.

The evidence is clear – Third Generation Leadership applications work and provide accountability – even when that accountability is required in monetary terms!

PART THREE
Create the Future

In which we consider the possible long term impacts of the leadership approaches that we need

12

Self-Confident People – the Effect of Third Generation Leadership

I was walking through a major Sydney shopping centre on a rainy afternoon in midwinter. The centre was fairly full of people and the retailers should have been pretty happy with the volume of floor traffic. I'm a 'people watcher' and I decided that having a cup of coffee so that I could unobtrusively observe the shoppers was a good idea. (Those who know me are fully aware that I can almost always find an excuse for a cup of good coffee!) I chose a coffee shop quite close to a pet store. Now I don't really like pet stores both because so many of them deal with animals bred in 'puppy farms' and the like and also because the very presence of pet stores can encourage emotional responses that result in many people buying puppies, kittens or other pets that they don't really want and that may later get abandoned or abused. However, this time I noticed that the pet shop was having an interesting and positive effect on shoppers.

From where I sat I could see people entering the shopping centre from the car park and most seemed to look quite dismal and disgruntled. Perhaps it was the time of year and the rain, but people looked grumpy and anxious. Even infants and young children seemed subdued and a bit sullen. Almost everyone seemed to head for the pet shop. Even if they were on the other side of the mall, most people seemed to cross over to look at the animals as they passed. Behind the glass the puppies were playing in the shredded paper that lined their cages. The puppies were full of the joy of being alive. They were being, well, puppies! And the effect on the shoppers was instant. Almost without exception, after watching the puppies for a few seconds, everyone moved on with a lighter step and a smile on their faces. Whatever the concerns people may have had, for a few moments these were dispelled as the puppies brought some light and sunshine.

At the heart of the human condition lies existential anxiety.[1] Essentially existential anxiety is a search for meaning in life. As such it is unique to humanity.

People who have appropriately dealt with their existential anxiety are people who have the ability to be self-confident. Self-confident people are those who understand that there is no need for any form of 'talking down to' or 'putting down of' other people. Self-confident people are those who always treat others with respect and who, as a result, ultimately expect to earn trust and respect for themselves – but they're not upset if, in the end, others fail to respect them. A self-confident person is one who is always cognisant of the fact that everyone has his or her own issues with which they have to deal. Sometimes a person's personal issues are such that their ability to ever trust and respect another is seriously impaired. Self-confidence is not weakness or any behaviour that indicates a lack of personal resolve. But neither is it the bold, brassy over-confidence that is encountered in the worst examples of some who seek to place unacceptable levels of pressure on people in order to achieve results. Self-confident people are those who have come to grips with their search for meaning in life. Self-confident people have watched the puppies play! Frequently!

For many years it seemed as though the search for meaning in life was not really an issue. To an extent, in the world of First Generation Leadership, this was true. But the Second World War placed an emphasis on the search for meaning such as had never existed before. Events such as the Holocaust made many question the very core of humanity itself. After the war, one concentration camp survivor, Victor Frankl,[2] brought to the fore the way in which he and others in concentration camps dealt with facing the constant threat of death and annihilation. Was life just a brief spasm with no ultimate purpose? Was life really worth living? What, really, is life all about? Victor Frankl, having worked through these issues while an inmate of a concentration camp, concluded that the meaning of life is found in every moment of living. He concluded that life never ceases to have meaning, even in suffering and death.

An old song[3] summarises this search for meaning as it concludes with the words:

---

1   'Existential Anxiety' was, I believe, a term first used by Paul Tillich in his 1952 book *The Courage To Be*, Yale University Press, USA.
2   Victor Frankl, *Man's Search for Meaning*, 1964 (first published 1946), Hodder & Stoughton Ltd, USA.
3   Written by Jerry Leiber and Mike Stoller and recorded by Peggy Lee in November 1969. The song was originally recorded by Leslie Uggams in 1968.

I know what you must be saying to yourselves,
if that's the way she feels about it why doesn't she just end it all?
Oh, no, not me. I'm in no hurry for that final disappointment,
for I know just as well as I'm standing here talking to you,
when that final moment comes and I'm breathing my last breath, I'll be saying
to myself
Is that all there is, is that all there is
If that's all there is my friends, then let's keep dancing
Let's break out the booze and have a ball
If that's all there is

Victor Frankl would have said, 'no, that's not all there is. Meaning is found in having a "why" to live – and the ultimate "why" to live is because somebody, somewhere, really cares'. And that, as we shall see, is a very Third Generation Leadership approach.

Traditionally people have found the answer to this quest for meaning in work and societal structure coupled with a philosophic or religious faith of one sort or another.

Over the years three main ways of dealing with existential anxiety have emerged and these correspond to First Generation Leadership, Second Generation Leadership and Third Generation Leadership.

First Generation Leadership enables a person to deal with at least some of their existential anxiety by following the rules (life is predictable). Under the First Generation Leadership approach people had a clear sense of purpose – to do exactly as they were told – and they knew that when they obeyed instructions their future was secure. Whether at work, in religion or in society at large, their sense of personal identity was tied up in knowing their place in society and in fulfilling the roles that were expected from their stratum. For most of them their work was able to be learned to the stage where the tasks became habits and so could be completed with little or no conscious thought. The same was true in the religious sphere. By learning rituals, prayers, chants and the like, religious duties could be performed with little or no conscious thought. The penalty for freethinking was excommunication, eternal damnation or death – something that is still a dominant theme in many religions and faiths today. Under such a regime for most people, in all areas of life, higher level learning, creativity and innovation were largely lacking and, for the vast majority of the population, actively discouraged.

Second Generation Leadership enables a person to deal with at least some of their existential anxiety by conformance to norms and rules and confidence in learning from experience. Under the Second Generation Leadership approach the blue zone started to be harnessed. In the Second Generation Leadership world people were encouraged to learn from experience and to think about what they were doing. Training was able to move from being rote learning and this gave rise to the tremendous increase in productivity and economic activity that we saw in the post-Second World War period. This was accompanied by a 'jobs for life' and 'cradle-to-grave social system' in countries such as the UK, Australia and New Zealand. Anxiety about the future was dealt with by conformance because, if one conformed to society's mores, there was total confidence that you would be cared for in your old age. The welfare society had its benefits.

At the same time, because Second Generation Leadership was an evolution from First Generation Leadership, the traditional First Generation Leadership approaches found in government, business, society and most religions and faiths could continue without being openly challenged.

In religion at least people continued to give some form of acquiescence to the dominant religious faith in their family, society or country. However, two phenomena appeared in relation to religious practice. On the one hand there was a significant incidence of 'nominal' faith – i.e. people who claimed allegiance to a particular faith or denomination but seldom, if ever, attended a place of worship. Simultaneously there was an increase of affiliation to a fundamentalist form of that faith. This is something that still continues today across a variety of faiths and denominations. Clearly the issue of existential anxiety was (and is) being resolved by people in different ways. For some the freedom to openly question and to deal with ambiguity and complexity (blue zone) has brought release from anxiety: for others this same freedom has brought about disquiet that could and can only be resolved by retreat into an obedience framework (red zone).

Third Generation Leadership enables a person to deal with at least some of their existential anxiety by realising that 'I matter to someone' and 'I am making a difference'. Self-confidence eventually develops because 'somebody cares'. As Victor Frankl's message put it, meaning is found in having a 'why' to live.

Third Generation Leadership has been emerging since the early 1980s but, unlike its immediate predecessor, it is a substantial change from the preceding phase and its emergence requires shifts in underlying thought processes and behaviour as well as changes in policies, technologies and training.

These underlying thought processes and behaviours are very persistent and explain the long delay in Third Generation Leadership becoming dominant. Simply, most leaders have been successful in their careers using the skills of 2G Leadership and operating within a Second Generation Leadership framework – their red zones of brain control are dominant and fully operational. A shift to 3G Leadership and a Third Generation Leadership world requires a huge change in one's thought processes and personal behaviours – a change that is difficult to make for people whose very success has been based on the behaviours that now need to change. Third Generation Leadership requires a change in behaviour such that every individual with whom the leader interacts comes to recognise that the leader is special and worthy of respect – and to people who 'demand' respect by virtue of their position, the thought of 'earning' respect is close to anathema.

Because First Generation Leadership and Second Generation Leadership both have the brain's locus of control ultimately in the red zone, the prospect of having to earn respect is deemed to be threatening. The 'red zone' is characterised by fear of what is a possible threat. As I have said, both First Generation Leadership and Second Generation Leadership are ultimately controlled from the 'red zone' which ensures that there is resistance to change – often very strong resistance. Thus, even as we make the tortuous transition to a Third Generation Leadership world, we encounter very real pressure to revert to the old ways of doing things. We want the security of doing what we've always done – even if the evidence is that it doesn't work – simply because there is comfort in it – 'this is the way we do things around here'.

To those operating from the traditional leadership perspectives, Third Generation Leadership is unsettling. By dealing with existential anxiety by means of ensuring every person knows that they matter; that they will be listened to; and that they are important in their own right, both the leaders and the followers are moved into new territory. The fact that we no longer have the security of knowing exactly what we have to do and how we have to do it challenges us to shift our Gravesian worldviews – and making such change has implications across every area of life. Many of us would prefer to not deal with these implications especially if it means a loss in our perceived power and authority.

In the macro environment of international relations, the complexity of today requires 'blue zone' thinking. The fiasco of the Israeli–Palestinian imbroglio; the tragedies of the Iraq and Afghanistan ventures; the problems in Africa and with both North Korea and Iran; the issue of illicit drugs and countless other world issues are proof that First Generation Leadership and Second Generation Leadership approaches have had their day. But if we can't resolve these problems and issues in the ways we used in the past and by which we are trying today, that's pretty scary – it means that we no longer have even the appearance of control and this perception of lack of control challenges the essence of our very beings – it leads to existential anxiety. No wonder we persist with approaches that, deep down, we know can only lead to failure.

But Third Generation Leadership is also critical in the personal sphere. One of the most common and debilitating illnesses today is clinical depression. Pharmaceutical companies make fortunes designing and selling antidepressant drugs and I suspect that a significant amount of alcohol use and illicit drug use is also to help people deal with the same issue.

Depression, in its most general sense, is a state of low mood and aversion to activity. It is a psychological disorder that affects an individual's mood changes, physical functions and social interactions. In its least severe form, a person may appear normal but he or she requires markedly increased effort to do anything. In its most severe form, a person with clinical depression can have changes in appetite or weight, difficulty sleeping, decreased energy, feelings of worthlessness or guilt, difficulty thinking, concentrating, or making decisions, or recurrent thoughts of death. Feeling 'depressed' is often synonymous with feeling 'sad', but both clinical depression and non-clinical depression can also refer to more than one emotion or feeling.

Depression is a very real and very complex disorder but, in summary, a depressed person generally experiences feelings of sadness which can then escalate to feelings of helplessness and hopelessness.

In January 2010, the *Scientific American* published an article entitled 'Depression's Evolutionary Roots'. In this they reported that:

- The brain's ability to enter a depressed state has been preserved throughout evolution, suggesting that depression is an adaptation.

- Depression promotes focused rumination about problems. People in this state of mind are better at solving complex social dilemmas.

- Effective therapies encourage patients to engage in rumination, allowing them to find solutions to their problems and end their depressive episode.

They also reported that:

> research in the US and other countries estimates that between 30 to 50 percent of people have met current psychiatric diagnostic criteria for major depressive disorder sometime in their lives.

No wonder the pharmaceutical companies invest so much time and effort into the antidepressant market! The *Scientific American* article goes on to say:

> This ... seems to pose an evolutionary paradox. The brain plays crucial roles in promoting survival and reproduction, so the pressures of evolution should have left our brains resistant to such high rates of malfunction. Mental disorders are generally rare—why isn't depression?

I believe that one answer as to why depression is not rare lies in the fact of red zone being the dominant area of brain control for most people (see Chapter 6) and in the matter of existential anxiety.

Anxiety is different from either fear or depression but is related to both. Anxiety covers a spectrum from a vague feeling of unease, through being 'a worrier', through to a range of anxiety disorders such as obsessive compulsive disorder and the like. Anxiety becomes a matter of concern when it prevents a person from living their life to the full – from performing in the manner that they should be able to, or the manner in which they would like to perform. Anxiety has been described as a multi-system response to a perceived danger or threat. The red zone perceives a threat and a person's biochemical balance changes with a view to escaping from the threat or of having the threat go away. Where fear is a direct, focused response to an immediate, specific threatening event or object and the person is very aware of this threat, anxiety is often unfocused, vague and hard to pin down to a specific cause. In this state we may well look dismal and disgruntled as did the shoppers I was watching while having my cup of coffee.

Existential anxiety is different from, although related to, anxiety in the clinical sense. As I have said, existential anxiety is all about one's sense of ultimate meaning. If people have an in-built desire to find meaning in their existence (and I strongly believe that they do) then those times when they are unable to find any such meaning will impact on how they feel and behave – anxiety in its general sense can occur. Unless this anxiety is alleviated, it may lead to a very real perception of threat (which engenders fear) and can eventually escalate. The impact of this uncertainty about a sense of real meaning in one's life will range from a general feeling of disquiet and 'feeling a bit down' through to clinical anxiety disorder and, sometimes, all the way to severe clinical depression – and the downward transition may occur extremely rapidly depending on the circumstances surrounding the person affected.

In a world in which there is almost total certainty – a First Generation Leadership world – the issue of depression is unlikely to be widespread. Because the emphasis is on 'doing what one is told' there is pressure to accept one's lot in life and, once this is accepted, existential anxiety is allayed. 'Don't rock the boat' would be an apt motto for this period.

In a world where there is a reasonable degree of certainty – a Second Generation Leadership world – there will be those who 'don't rock the boat' as well as those who use (either overtly or covertly) the freedom to question and this will impact on their lives. In its most positive form, this questioning will lead to a feeling of disquiet about whatever it is they are questioning and, in turn, that will lead to creativity and innovation. Such a progression is in accord with the findings reported by the *Scientific American* when they said 'Depression promotes focused rumination about problems. People in this state of mind are better at solving complex social dilemmas'. It is no accident that the post-Second World War period saw some of the greatest advances the world has ever known in work productivity, economic activity and technology.

But in its negative form, this questioning can lead to serious psychological and physical health problems.

I have no doubt that anxiety in one form or another has always existed in humans. Additionally, I am quite sure that 'depression' as an illness existed before the 1980s but I strongly suspect that the incidence of depression has accelerated since the onset of the Third Generation Leadership era. The reason is simple. The advent of personal computing coupled with the availability of the Internet and, now, social networking sites such as LinkedIn, Plaxo,

Facebook, Twitter, etc. means people are faced with a level of complexity and choice with which many of them are unable to cope. For those educated in the years up to 1980 questioning and 'thinking outside the square' was either actively discouraged or allowed only under controlled circumstances. The trick was to ascertain what those in authority wanted and then to show conformance with this. The key task was to second-guess the boss. But second-guessing one's leaders is a game of 'survivor' and only the best (or, more usually, the most cunning) make it through all of the challenges. Unless extremely well 'connected', very few people have 'immunity'! When loss of certainty occurs or the available options appear to be too many, existential anxiety rears its head and a high probability result is depression.

To summarise my argument here, from time to time, people who have been perfectly comfortable with how things are become aware of something dissonant – anxiety occurs. They may not be able to identify it, but it has an impact on them. It could be said that the person 'feels sad'. From here there are two possible paths – the first is the path of positive change to a new stable situation which may involve innovation and creativity; the second is to remain 'sad' and to encounter the possibility of going further down the track of depression. In this latter situation it is almost certain that, unless some positive action is taken and/or help is provided, eventually professional psychiatric, medical, psychological and/or similar professional help will be necessary.

This can be related to the issue of depression in its broadest form and also linked with the statements made above from the *Scientific American*. Anxiety can produce positive advances as well as having negative impacts.

What is involved here is the issue of change. Change is central to leadership. With First Generation Leadership and Second Generation Leadership, leaders had far greater control over things – 'command and control' was the dominant (or fallback) emphasis – and, for those under their charge, leaders could restrict access to or understanding of the external environment. With Third Generation Leadership this control is simply not possible. (If you doubt this, then consider the impact of such organisations as WikiLeaks who obtain and release information governments and other authorities would far rather remain 'secret'.) As a result change must come in the leader him or herself.

The *Scientific American* article makes it clear that an early aspect of depression can lead to creativity. A person feels 'down' or suffers some disquiet about his or her situation and, under the right circumstances, can use this disquiet to develop new approaches – the experience is used to harness their creative ability. This is a 'blue zone' activity and 3G Leaders are adept at helping people shift their brain's locus of control into the 'blue zone'. Their tools for doing this are:

- powerful questioning;

- observational listening;

- optimistic listening.

As discussed earlier (Chapter 9) a wonderful side effect of this process is that not only is the follower helped move into the blue zone, but even a First Generation Leader or a Second Generation Leader who uses this approach eventually finds him or herself in the blue zone as well.

Does this mean that with the development of a Third Generation Leadership world and the rise of 3G Leaders we will abolish anxiety and depression? Not at all. What is does mean, however, is that in a Third Generation Leadership world an increasing number of people will find that their leaders are able to facilitate brain control shift – from red zone to blue zone – and that this shift will help individuals deal with the issue of anxiety in a positive way. Such a shift will also help those clinicians providing professional services relating to anxiety and depression as there will be a more supportive environment into which their patients can return.

We all know that many of today's problems are the result of yesterday's solutions. First Generation Leadership and Second Generation Leadership have proven themselves to be incapable of correcting yesterday's and today's situations. The result is ongoing and increasing tensions on the international scene and increasing amounts of despair and depression on the individual front. It is clear that a red zone control is incapable of giving us the world we want tomorrow.

We need Third Generation Leadership and 3G Leaders. Third Generation Leadership develops self-confident people. Self-confident people are those who know that they matter to other people. Self-confident people are those people who have the resilience to face whatever is thrown at them. Self-confident people are secure in the knowledge that there is a way forward and they are confident in their ability (and in the ability of those around them) to find Third

Generation Leadership answers to Third Generation Leadership issues in a Third Generation Leadership world.

Each of us can be, and each of us should be, a self-confident person. A key tool in helping more people become self-confident is Third Generation Leaders (3G Leaders) in a Third Generation Leadership world. While puppies can help people allay anxiety for a few moments, Third Generation Leadership can help people for a far longer period.

But before we consider the shift to a Third Generation Leadership world there are three other areas at which we must look – areas that are of vital interest to almost every one of us.

13

Dealing with the Recalcitrant!

Lois was appointed CEO of an organisation employing 680 people and with annual turnover in excess of $100 million. Patricia, the general manager (operations), had been an internal applicant for the CEO's role but she was fully prepared to remain in her existing role when Lois was appointed. Lois has found Patricia to be a tireless worker who produces results.

After about a year of getting to know the organisation intimately, Lois decided that the culture of the organisation needed changing. Her observations showed clearly that there was room for improvement in all areas. Lois was supported in this by the chairman and board.

Without knowing about Third Generation Leadership, Lois embarked on a programme to make the organisation more collegial and inclusive. One of her first symbolic changes was to operate an open door policy in which any employee could access her easily. To facilitate this she moved her executive assistant to an office adjoining the CEO's office. The effect of this was to make it possible for anyone entering the executive area to immediately see whether or not Lois was available. This was a marked contrast from the approach taken by previous CEOs and it soon became clear that the shift was noticed and appreciated by most staff. Lois added to this by being very active in moving around the organisation and no one was quite sure when she would turn up and chat with them. Initially there was suspicion and apprehension about these visits but by part-way through her second year suspicion had gone; Lois was widely respected and she was warmly welcomed no matter where she went.

This open door policy and these visits did not mean that Lois tried to interfere in the work done by her executives and she was always careful to ensure that the executive team was fully in the loop as to what she was doing. When she became aware of matters requiring attention Lois was meticulous in ensuring that the appropriate channels were used to address them. However it had quickly become apparent to everyone that Lois knew exactly what was going on across the organisation. This meant that reports could no longer gloss over anything in order to make any particular person or group look either 'good' or 'bad'.

On the surface, Patricia was quite comfortable with this. She supported Lois' initiatives for training everyone in the new approach and was enthusiastic about the changes when talking with directors, fellow executives and people both within and outside of the company. However clearly she was experiencing some internal conflict and this showed in her micro-managing of the areas under her charge. Where Lois wanted to encourage decision-making at the lowest possible level and to encourage an atmosphere of innovation, Patricia wanted to know every last detail of everything in order to ensure that there was nothing Lois might learn that wasn't already known to Patricia. No significant decision could be made without first consulting Patricia. In addition Patricia moved to appoint to key roles only people who would support her and who would report to her everything that was happening. The result was a steady decline in respect for Patricia and the development of a 'don't let Patricia or her spies know about this' culture from her reports.

Lois became increasingly worried about this. She valued Patricia's contribution and wanted her to stay with the organisation but the situation couldn't be allowed to continue. Lois said to me, 'how can I deal with someone who doesn't seem to really want to make the shift to a new culture?'.

This issue of reluctance to change is probably the most common matter encountered in any change initiative. There are two key things to remember when dealing with it:

- Remember what Clare Graves said (Chapter 7) – people don't 'have' to change. Ultimately the decision as to whether or not a person wants to develop a new worldview is a choice that only each individual can make for him or herself.

- Remember that willingness to change behaviour is very difficult when a person has been successful with behaviours that are no longer appropriate (Chapter 8).

I have made the point before that resistance to change comes out of the brain's red zone area of control. Clearly Patricia, no matter how much she tried to support a 'blue zone' approach, found that she was dominated by her red zone. It is in this understanding of the brain's area of control that we find the clues to dealing with people who appear to undermine the change process.

When you are 'the boss' it's not too difficult to deal with this sort of situation. Lois explained her concerns to Patricia and it was agreed that I would work with her. The starting point with Patricia was to visit the 'blue zone–red zone' concept and this was followed by cognitive coaching. Given the right environment and appropriate support, Patricia was able to adapt to the new approach.

But how does one deal with the situation when it is a peer, your boss, or the overall organisational culture that fails to see and/or support a Third Generation Leadership approach? This becomes a test of one's commitment to a Third Generation Leadership world. It is also where much of the learning from the leadership research of the twentieth century comes into play.

From twentieth-century research we know that any person can lead from any position in any organisation. Even in a family, how often do children take the lead in getting parents to do what the child wants? Leadership is not dependent upon one's place in a hierarchy. It is this fact that enables informal organisational structures to be so influential in affecting organisational culture and performance. The twentieth century also taught us that, at its core, leadership is the generic concept of influence. These two pieces of knowledge converge when we lack positional power but we need to deal with people who are slow to enter the Third Generation Leadership world and/or who oppose the development of a Third Generation Leadership world. The starting point is to focus on *my* behaviour rather than to focus on the behaviour of the other person – to focus on *my* performance, not theirs (see Figure 2.5 on page 31).

For many years counsellors have known the strength of 'I' statements – those statements which let others know how 'I' am feeling or concerns 'I' may have. These are statements which remove threat and encourage all parties to move into the blue zone. In Chapter 8 I spoke of the need to create a safe zone before development can commence. 'I' statements help create this safe zone in which discussion can take place without fear. In this environment positive resolution of an issue becomes possible.

By focusing on my performance and explaining difficulties I may be having in reaching my performance goals the emphasis moves away from how 'the other' should change to how 'the other' can help me achieve whatever it is I am supposed to achieve. After all, I cannot control whether or not 'the other' adopts a Third Generation Leadership approach – but I can use a Third Generation Leadership approach in my interaction with him or her or 'them'. Now it is an easy step for me to set out what support I need or would like from 'the other' in order for me to perform.

When this is done, influencing can start. Working out of my own blue zone and sharing my concerns about my performance I open the door for genuine dialogue. Through applying the techniques discussed in Chapter 9 (powerful questioning, observational listening, optimistic listening) I show respect for the other person and simultaneously I show both that they are being listened to, and that I have belief in the other person. Such behaviour from me optimises the probability that the other person will either move to or remain in their blue zone.

Again, however, it is essential to always remember:

- what Clare Graves said (Chapter 7) – people don't 'have' to change. Ultimately the decision as to whether or not a person wants to develop a new worldview is a choice that only each individual can make for him or herself; and

- that willingness to change behaviour is very difficult when a person has been successful with behaviours that are no longer appropriate (Chapter 8).

Accordingly dealing with those who are reluctant to change may take quite a long time. And that is true no matter what the context in which we are trying to exercise leadership.

14

Third Generation Leadership Families

When she was about 18, my youngest daughter, Michelle, commented one day that some of her friends seemed envious of the relationship Michelle had with us, her parents. She said how one friend had made the statement that, in the past three years, she could not remember giving her mother a spontaneous hug. Apparently the mother of another friend also commented that she found it almost unbelievable that Michelle would want to spend time with her parents. Now one thing for certain, Michelle was no different from her friends in relation to partying and having a good time. She could (and did) party with the best of them and staying out late or all night was not uncommon. She loved spending time with her friends. But Michelle also loves spending time with her parents. And that is certainly *not* because we were wealthy or flush with money and could give our children everything they wanted! She loved spending time with her parents because Michelle had reaped the benefit of what we, her parents, had been taught by her siblings.

'Family' is important to me and to most people I know, or have ever known. I define a family as being, at the minimum, a parent (whether or not a natural parent) and a child. Of course 'family' can then expand from this minimum to embrace partner or spouse (no matter what gender), siblings and then to other generations of the same family group such as grandparents, great grandparents, aunts, uncles, cousins, etc. – the extended family concept.

Sometimes in the whole discussion about leadership it seems that leadership in a family situation is either forgotten or largely ignored. Yet leadership in a family situation is probably the single most important leadership role any person can hold. Leadership in the family situation is also the only leadership role that has always been independent of one's stratum in society – virtually every person is potentially a parent and hence potentially also a leader.

I know that myriad books have been written about parenting and numerous experts will and do provide recipes for having a 'good' family situation. I'm no expert – but I do have five children and, over the years, I have made a lot of mistakes. I have learned a lot about developing relationships with one's children and having positive family relationships. I have become totally convinced that the key to positive family relationships lies in applying Third Generation Leadership principles and operating from the brain's blue zone locus of control. It was not always so. I had to learn most of this the hard way – fortunately, at least for most of the time, my children were prepared to work with me.

There seems to be an inherent human characteristic for us to 'parent as we were parented'. As with every other aspect of leadership today, this means that because most of us were parented in a First Generation Leadership or a Second Generation Leadership manner, we tend to perpetuate this approach. For many years I was no different.

When I was a child the phrase 'children should be seen but not heard' was an oft repeated refrain. We learned that our role was to obey and that message was reinforced by the larger family, society at large, the Bible and corporal punishment. Mine was not some abusive family who didn't care for their children – to the contrary. We were loved and cared for by parents who were genuinely concerned for us and who wanted us to be everything that we could be – fulfilling one's potential was stressed to all of us. But we were brought up, as were our peers, in the society of the time – a First Generation Leadership world. My parents had also been brought up in a First Generation Leadership world and, at least until the late 1950s, they recognised the realities of this First Generation Leadership world and they sought to equip me and my siblings for living in the same.

This was a world where in order to go to the shops one would 'dress properly' – no old clothes for going 'down town'! This was a world in which, on a Sunday, everyone would be dressed in their 'Sunday best' and taken off to church where, no matter how boring the service, one would need to sit still and not go to sleep. This was a world in which, on a Sunday afternoon, parents might decide that the family should go and visit friends and relatives, and so, having dressed appropriately, the family would go and see some other family. Once there we would be told we may 'look but do not touch' any of the ornaments or other items to be found. It was just as bad if we stayed at home and others came to visit us. Children were expected to sit quietly unless told that they may go outside and play or, if the parents so desired, they were expected to show off appropriate entertainment skills by singing or doing some other activity to 'entertain the visitors while [Mother] went to organise afternoon tea'. No such thing as TV or video games in those days!

Don't get me wrong. I'm not complaining. This was simply the way things were in those days of the 1940s and 1950s and, from my recollection, our family was not really much different from any other family.

In terms of the Gravesian model (Chapter 7), this was a parenting world in which Level 1.2 (family or tribe), Level 1.3 (power) and Level 1.4 (one best way) ruled. There were very few areas of ambiguity and relatively low levels of complexity. As children we all knew, and fitted in with, our place in society. The brain's red zone locus of control was firmly in place for everyone.

Young parents of today grew up in a different world. My older daughters were born in the early to mid 1970s and this was very definitely a Second Generation Leadership world (even if I was still a First Generation Leadership parent!).

By the 1970s the concept of 'operant conditioning'[1] had become fairly well known and practised. The intention of operant conditioning is to encourage voluntary conformance with whatever behaviour is desired through making it clear that all behaviour has consequences and that the 'good' consequences – rewards – are far preferable to the opposite. For many people this concept says that one should reward good behaviour while punishing inappropriate behaviour. In the Second Generation Leadership children were expected to conform to family norms and to parental controls – such conformance would be rewarded while failure to conform (obey?) brought punishment. This was the world for my older children. Again, as with previous generations, overall those responsible for bringing up children did a remarkably good job. Sure there were exceptions, but the vast majority of parents and carers of the 1960s and 1970s should be congratulated for the way their children have matured into responsible adults – or the children should be congratulated for having overcome the way in which they were brought up!

The downside of these First Generation Leadership and Second Generation Leadership approaches to parenting and to family life lies in the issue of control. Both First Generation Leadership and Second Generation Leadership

---

1   There is a very good discussion of this concept on Wikipedia.

are predicated on some form of power-based hierarchy and control. Today many parents of young children still seem to be in this mindset.

One area in which I have observed this First and Second Generation Leadership aspect as being of concern is that of perinatal depression. First Generation Leadership and Second Generation Leadership approaches are ill-equipped to deal with ambiguity and high levels of complexity. While this has always been the case, in recent years there have been many women who have chosen to develop a career before starting a family. There is absolutely nothing wrong with this. However, today's dominant workplace paradigm is still one of controlling people and events through various management and leadership practices. Uncertainty and an apparent inability to deal with ambiguity and complexity are seen as 'career limiting' for the ambitious young person – whether male or female. The result is that ambiguity and uncertainty are ignored, disguised or reduced to some point where a relatively simple solution can be imposed.

Introduce a baby into this world and suddenly ambiguity and complexity abound whether or not we are equipped to deal with them. And now this ambiguity and complexity can't be ignored!

From a purely physiological perspective, pregnancy and childbirth brings physical, hormonal and emotional changes. This is natural and something which should be (and generally is) understood and accepted by the vast majority of people. But it can have a negative psychological impact – perinatal depression.

This new little person – someone who, in almost every instance, is keenly anticipated, deeply and strongly loved, and for whom the new parent(s) wants nothing but the best – has a mind of his, her (or their!) own. When hunger hits, baby cries. When there is physical discomfort, baby cries. When there is illness or injury, baby cries. When tiredness comes, baby cries. Too cold? Baby cries. Hungry, thirsty? Baby cries. In these very early days and weeks it seems as though only two stages exist for baby – comfortable (or asleep) and quiet or something wrong and crying. And knowing what baby is trying to communicate when crying is not always easy.

In the workplace, if your follower doesn't respond how you'd like them to, ultimately a separation can occur – either you initiate it or they do! As part of this separation process, almost certainly there will be discussions and both sides can have some form of dialogue that is understood (even if not accepted) by both parties. This isn't possible with baby! Here, verbal communication is only one way – from baby! And often we parents don't know what baby is saying. 'Sacking' baby, of course, is totally out of the question for most people.

Talk about ambiguity and complexity! For a new mother who wants to do everything 'just right' this can be a daunting and threatening experience. To combat any feelings of inadequacy, some authorities talk about the need to make the baby conform to your programme. There are some who argue baby should be fed, bathed and generally cared for at set times – even if that means waking baby from normal sleep. But sometimes baby doesn't want to fit in with 'Mum' and/or 'Dad' (in same-sex relationships obviously these terms may not be totally appropriate but they are used for convenience). Sometimes baby persists in demanding that Mum and/or Dad themselves adapt. This can be a challenge to the worldview Mum and Dad hold. Baby is saying that a Gravesian Level 1.1 world (basic survival) demands others adapt to him or her. This can be a challenge to a parent's Gravesian Level 1.4 (one best way) worldview. When to this mix is added a lack of sleep and a degree of physical exhaustion a potentially explosive mixture results. As I said in Chapter 12, the result can be anxiety and, in the worst cases, depression – here perinatal depression.

Again as I said in Chapter 12, a Third Generation Leadership approach – developing the skills to operate from the brain's blue zone where one is best able to deal with ambiguity and complexity – can be of tremendous help here. A spouse, partner, close friend or relative with Third Generation Leadership skills has the potential to provide health saving and, possibly, relationship saving facilitation. However, if one is locked into a First Generation Leadership or a Second Generation Leadership mindset with one's brain's locus of control reverting to the red zone from perceived threat, and no help is available, strife is imminent and relationship breakdown may well ensue – sometimes to the extent of harm to baby or oneself – or both.

The situation of ambiguity and complexity doesn't get any easier as baby develops into an infant, child, adolescent and young adult (even though perinatal depression may be long past). Each stage is accompanied by different challenges – especially as the child starts to develop his or her own conceptual skills which may eventually move to the point of questioning the very fabric of his or her parents' value system and life practices.

Andrew Mowat said in his chart (Chapter 7) 'Every person today can be engaged by a Leader 3.0, some by a Leader 2.0 and few by a Leader 1.0'. In other words, only Third Generation Leadership has the power to enable parents to navigate these years in a manner that has a high probability of engaging children through this entire period and maintaining strong, positive relationships despite all the changes and turmoil. Families need Third Generation Leadership.

Like many others, I had to learn this shift to the blue zone the hard way. I had to learn that we move towards this blue zone of control through the concept of respect. Respect in the family starts with respect between the parents or caregivers. They are the model that will have the greatest impact on the children in the family.

Over the years, my understanding and practice of leadership in the family situation has developed to the stage where I now believe the ideal family is one in which there is a true partnership between the parents or caregivers. In this situation there is no hierarchy – both partners are equal when it comes to all aspects of authority and caregiving and, as far as is biologically possible, tasks to be done are done by either parent. Both partners fully accept their shared leadership role in which they work as a team of fully equal partners to nurture and care for their children. Unfortunately my observations also indicate that this is a relatively rare situation.

I look at families today and all too often I see some form of bullying of one partner by the other and, in far too many cases, I see this degenerate to an aspect of dysfunctionality in which mental and/or physical abuse occurs – sometimes to the point of serious criminality. The causes of this abuse are many and varied and, all too often, include substance abuse of one or another form – but underlying them is an inadequate amount of self-confidence in one or both partners and an inability to deal with the degree of ambiguity and complexity that exists in any parenting situation. In these situations true mutual and unconditional respect is all but impossible. Yet children need unconditional respect if they are to grow into psychologically sound adolescents, young people and adults.

Like many others, I had to learn about unconditional respect towards my children. I had to re-learn what I had first been told many years before 'ultimately, its not what you wear on your shoulders that's important – it's what holds it up there!'. Just as in the Army I'd had to learn how to earn respect from the soldiers, as a parent I had to learn how to earn the respect of my children.

As a Third Generation Leader in a parenting role or in a family situation, respect goes through a cycle of three clear stages. When a baby is very small, unconditional respect is essential and generally very obviously provided. Baby cannot do anything for him or herself and cannot even communicate clearly and easily as to what he or she wants and needs. When dealing with a baby (at a Gravesian Level 1.1 stage (basic survival)) every aspect of care and support has to be initiated by the leader and it must always be assumed that 'baby knows best'. This unconditional respect says 'no matter what you do, I will always love you and care for you'. Most parents have no difficulty in understanding and applying this.

The situation changes as the infant starts to develop cognition. Once an infant can begin to understand something about what they are doing, a developing version of unconditional respect is appropriate. For many parents, this change becomes most apparent with the outbreak of 'the terrible twos'!

Now there is a tendency for parents to tell the child it is 'naughty'. This is the time when, for many parents, some form of punishment is introduced. What the parent wants is total compliance with the parent's wishes. The problems, from the child's perspective, are that, first, the child may not yet fully understand what the parent is saying and, second, that the child is simultaneously developing its own sense of identity. This developing sense of identity may not be at the stage that the parent would like.

And accompanying this 'naughty' complaint, many parents also provide punishments of one sort or another. The range of these punishments can be from as simple as a raised voice through to shouting and screaming, through to psychological and physical violence – not necessarily in that order. It is at this stage that, for many children, the scene is set for later becoming dysfunctional adolescents and adults. Does that parent usually genuinely care for the child no matter how the parent responds to 'naughtiness'? In most cases 'yes'. Does the parent genuinely love the child? Again, in most cases 'yes'. Does the parent want to give the child that which is best for the child? Again, in most cases 'yes'. In other words, most times when a parent punishes a child there is nothing but love behind the action. Invariably parental such action is taken 'for your own good'![2]

---

2   Readers interested in more information about this issue may like to refer to Alice Miller, *For Your Own Good*, 1990, Farrar, Straus and Giroux, New York.

But is the punishment effective? In other words, does the punishment have the long-term effect of changing behaviour while simultaneously encouraging mental and emotional growth and personal accountability? Bearing in mind that both rewards and punishment come out of the brain's red zone, I believe the answer generally is 'no'. From my own experience and from that of every person with whom I have discussed this issue, it is clear that the main effect of such punishment is that the person being punished takes a further step along the road to 'don't get caught' with every punishment received. It's a little like aversion therapy. Talking with people who have had aversion therapy, they all tell me they didn't learn to hate the behaviour for which they were treated – but they certainly learned to hate the therapist! The seeds for potentially poor relationships between parent and child are sown at this stage and, for too many families, these seeds later develop.

The older I have got, the more convinced I have become that, in the long term, punishment (any punishment for anything) seldom, if ever, really works the way we intend it to. I am also aware that rewards can equally be self-defeating. Once a person starts to have access to their brain's blue zone area of control, operant conditioning ceases to be an effective tool.

The problem is that punishment and operant conditioning both come out of the red zone. A parent (or other responsible adult) operating out of Clare Graves' Level 1.4 (one best way) wants a particular behaviour from the other person. A failure to provide that behaviour is seen as a threat to 'how things should be done'. Red zone reacts to threat by fight, flight or freeze. In the red zone our choices are limited and our ability to deal with ambiguity and complexity is seriously impaired. The red zone – punishment – simply concentrates on getting rid of what we don't want and does little or nothing to bring about what we actually do want.

In many instances, operant conditioning is a powerful tool for getting what we do want. What operant conditioning says is that we should be demonstrating the behaviour we want and rewarding the child when he or she provides that behaviour. We should concentrate on getting what we want rather than on getting rid of what we don't want. And, in the long term, only unconditional respect coming from the blue zone will enable us to do this.

The critical issue with a child is that, no matter what his or her behaviour, the child needs to know that he or she is *always* totally acceptable *as a person*.

As with virtually every other aspect of performance, in my experience it is not that children and young people don't want to do the right thing – its not that they don't want to give desired performance – more often it's a case of not knowing how to give the desired performance. As a person grows and develops various physical, emotional and hormonal changes occur. These changes can impact on our thinking processes and create degrees of conflict between what we want to do and what we are able to do. The result can be that, even though we know what we should do, we actually do something different.

In a child this is a major issue. Conditional respect – the 'normal' way in which most of us deal with children – says I will only show respect to you as a person when and if you do what I want you to. In other words, I will respect you if you perform in the manner I want you to. This can be devastating to a child. A child needs to know that, whether or not he or she behaves as we would like them to, as a person they are still totally accepted and respected.

This unconditional respect can only become our default way of operating when we have our brain's locus of control firmly in the blue zone. It is only our default way of operating when we have fully embraced a Third Generation Leadership worldview and approach.

If we want strong, healthy families we need leaders – parents – with Third Generation Leadership understanding and behaviour. And the same is true in the education arena – which is where this journey began for me. The work led by John Corrigan[3] ascertained first what made 'great' teachers (i.e. that approximately 5 per cent of teachers that each of us can remember as having had a profound and positive impact on our education) different, then, second, facilitating a culture shift in schools such that these desired behaviours became the norm. As the research and experience in both Australia and in England shows, if we want a strong healthy education system we need teachers with Third Generation Leadership understanding and behaviour.

---

3   See the Appendix for more information about this.

15

Third Generation Leadership in the Workplace

Every business today is under increasing pressure to increase its profits. Every workplace is under pressure to achieve desired results. Read any stock market report and look at the stock valuations of any company you please, and it is clear that failure to meet the market's expectation in relation to profit is a recipe for falling stock price and the demise of a CEO.

Over the years of First Generation Leadership and Second Generation Leadership approaches we have developed tried and true ways of cutting costs, increasing sales and, in general, maximising productivity from every employee. The purpose of these is to minimise costs and optimise profits. Virtually every business school graduate learns the importance of these measures and we see it implemented with monotonous regularity. I outlined these measures in Chapter 4 when I said that the era of Second Generation Leadership seems to follow a predictable pattern (see Table 4.1, on page 51).

Today we need to find an approach that moves beyond 'shifting the deck chairs on the *Titanic'*. The Third Generation Leadership environment that is emerging with the increasing power and demands from Gen Y requires that we find a Third Generation Leadership approach to this whole issue of meeting the market's expectations relating to growth and profitability.

This was the issue that, at a workshop I conducted, prompted someone to ask 'How can Third Generation Leadership increase my organisation's profitability?'. It's a very important question. The answer is simple. The answer lies in trust and engagement. The answer lies in changing our leadership behaviour away from the Level 1.5 (excel) and Level 1.3 (power) worldview of Clare Graves' Spiral Dynamics (see Chapter 7) in which success is seen primarily as equated with wealth, power and control. The answer lies in enhancing commitment and cooperation by everyone so that they all work towards achievement of desired results. The answer lies in managing down our red zones and bringing about blue zone locus of brain control as our default position.

Improved profitability can be obtained through a very simple, yet very comprehensive process that is capable of harnessing the energies of everyone in the organisation. That is the message that has been propounded extensively through the earlier chapters. This increased profitability can be obtained through implementing the model provided in Chapter 2 – but doing this in a Third Generation Leadership manner.

In Chapter 2, I introduced a model (see Figure 2.5 on page 31) that emphasised the role of the leader as being that of an integrator and empowerer of the various factors that impact on organisational success. I stressed that performance is essential to every organisation – be it a family, a family group, business, or any other and/or of any size. The role of the leader is to make this performance possible and to encourage the commitment and engagement of every person in the attaining of this performance.

Underlying this model is the need for a leader to trust all the people he or she works with – not just the managers. When this trust exists – and it can only fully exist when the organisation is seeking to provide a Third Generation Leadership environment – it becomes possible to work with everyone in a very open manner in which everything is 'on the table'. As I say, the process for this is simple – but it is also very comprehensive.

The process I use with organisations involves group meetings in which everyone is asked to:

1.   Make a list of all the things that impact on your organisation's ability to operate profitably.

2.   Sort the list into two groups – those things within your organisation and those things external to your organisation.

3.   Sort the 'internal' list into the following categories: knowledge, strategy, non-human resources, structure, human process.

4.   Very honestly and as impartially as possible, assess each item in each category of this list as to whether it actively enhances

profitability, impedes profitability (usually by causing a problem or blockage that affects some other item from functioning effectively), or operates in such a way as to prevent profitability.

5. Determine how to rid your organisation of those things that prevent profitability and clear the impediments.

6. Determine how those items enhancing profitability can be further supported.

7. Sort the 'external' list into the following categories: those you can influence, those you cannot influence.

8. Develop a very clear plan for positively influencing each item you can influence and develop an approach for coping with those items you cannot influence.

9. Empower everyone to make the new plan work.

A First Generation Leader or a Second Generation Leader will try to control the discussion which evolves from the making of these lists because such a leader will see as a threat any suggestions which question the leader's thought process and preferred approach. Such leaders will make it clear that some items are not open for consideration. This is a red zone approach.

A Third Generation Leader will operate from his or her brain's blue zone of control. This will allow full engagement with everyone involved and enable new and creative solutions and approaches to be developed. Then by trusting people to actually implement what they have worked on developing, their commitment and competence will be harnessed towards achieving what needs to be done.

Depending on the size of your organisation you may need to cascade this down through a number of levels. Wherever possible, work in groups that cross organisational levels – if you bring all the executives together or all the managers together (or any other specific group) there is the risk that the group's thinking will conform to what has been done in the past or what they see as 'acceptable'. Of course, if you bring a wider spread of people into each group it is essential that there is total freedom to say what is really thought – and only a Third Generation Leader can fully create this environment. Let's consider how this worked in a real situation.

'New-way Corporation' was a manufacturing company. When I became involved it employed approximately 1,100 people and operated a seven-day, 24-hour operation using five shifts of factory workers. Virtually all employees were members of a powerful trade union. Where initially New-way had no local competition, the success of its operations meant increasing competition from both imports and new local producers. This increased competition, accompanied by an international economic downturn, created a situation in which, for two years, profits had fallen and despite all the usual methods of cost-cutting, there was no obvious solution to this profitability issue. The company's owners (located in the United States) then issued an edict that New-way return to the desired level of profit within the current year or the entire management team would be replaced and consideration would be given to closing New-way.

In talking with friends, New-way's CEO, Ian, became aware that I was advocating a different approach from the Second Generation Leadership system that was part of the culture of both New-way and its parent. He decided that it was at least worth investigating and, following discussions, a series of meetings were called at which all employees and their union representatives could be made aware of the situation. At these meetings Ian openly shared the edict from New-way's parent and he also shared his frustration at now knowing that previously successful ways of returning a company to profitability had not worked and showed no sign of working in the near future. He made it very clear that he was open to suggestions and input from anyone and everyone who had a vested interest in returning the company to profitability. He asked that everyone consider the situation over a one-week period and that then, either individually or as groups, they submit suggestions as to a way forward. Ian promised that all suggestions received would be shared and that they would all receive serious attention.

When the suggestions were received, it was clear that Ian's concern about the future of New-way was shared by everyone. Among the suggestions were several that suggested some form of committee of employees to work on the problem. Ian responded positively to this and a committee was formed comprising 11 people – five management and six non-management (including the secretary of the trade union representing most of the staff). It was agreed that Ian should chair this committee but that he would be included as one of the five management people. It was also agreed that decisions of the committee would be by consensus and that implementation of all decisions would be tried if at all possible. Committee members were tasked with both representing all employees to the committee as well as taking back to all employees the deliberations and decisions of the committee. The committee then followed the nine-step process outlined above.

Twelve months later New-way had not only returned to profitability but it was in the process of doubling its premises and had increased its staff to approximately 1,950 people. Five years after this, when New-way's US-based parent suffered a serious downturn in profitability, New-way was sold for a very significant capital gain. The new owners were clearly not attuned to Third Generation Leadership approaches and reintroduced a traditional structure and management approach by incorporating New-way into another business. Today New-way does not exist as an entity in its own right. However, both Ian and others who were part of New-way are still adamant that it was the Third Generation Leadership approach which brought about the shift back to growth and profitability. As Ian told me recently, the shift to Gravesian second tier thinking (process or integrated systems – Chapter 7), coupled with a blue-zone mindset, were the keys to success.

As this example indicates, there can be risks associated with a Third Generation Leadership approach! In New-way's case there was a failure to recognise that success could mean the owners might sell a successful, highly profitable operation. This was never considered as part of the external environmental factors and, in retrospect, Ian believes that this omission arose because the emphasis was on an urgent return to profitability rather than on possible subsequent actions of New-way's owners.

An organisation doesn't need to be in a crisis in order to implement a Third Generation Leadership approach – although as has been said, the threat of imminent disaster certainly has a way of focusing one's mind on change. As New-way discovered, the problem with making any major change under pressure is that some important items may not receive the attention that they need.

There is a significant advantage in making the shift at an early stage. Moving to a Third Generation Leadership approach at an early stage enables any organisation to properly implement a great concept that was developed during the Second Generation Leadership era – the concept of 'teams'.

For decades – at least since the 1980s – management theorists and management practitioners have been advocating organisations move to a team approach. The argument is, quite rightly, that teams have the potential to achieve synergy through harnessing everyone's energy and ability. Use the search engine of your choice and the Internet will provide you with millions of articles about, comments on, approaches to, and training programmes for, implementing a team approach. We have been regaled with aphorisms such as 'a champion team will always beat a team of champions' and we have been exhorted to use myriad sporting examples as models for a team approach.

Despite all of this there are grounds for believing that 'teams' is one of the most abused terms currently found in the management literature. Virtually all the research shows that teams can work. However, simultaneously the management literature shows that teams seldom work as effectively as they could. Our existing leadership practices are to blame.

First Generation Leadership never entertained the idea of teams. First Generation Leadership had rigidly hierarchical organisations with power centralised at the top. The role of subordinates was strictly one of obedience and, because the manager was seen as the source of knowledge, the issue of teams never arose. In general, Second Generation Leadership didn't really like the term 'subordinates' and sought to use other terms to describe the relationships in the hierarchy. The term 'reports' became a common one – even if the meaning remained the same – after all, the hierarchy was still there and power was still effectively centralised at the top. But now a new concept developed: that of teams.

Organisations with First Generation Leadership and/or Second Generation Leadership approaches (i.e. today's dominant organisational model) face a conflict of interest in relation to teams – especially if they try to introduce self-directed teams. By definition these organisations have a defined power structure and those people who want career advancement know that, no matter what the rhetoric, the fact is that the team needs to fit in with what is really wanted by 'the boss' – whether or not 'the boss' makes his or her real wishes clear – hidden agendas are common.

Today, at least in the Western world, most people operate in reasonably stable working conditions. No matter what generation of leadership is dominant, in every organisation there are goals to be reached and deadlines that must be met and there are parameters within which people should operate. But, in the main, these are known and accepted. People join an organisation because they believe that they will be able to make a contribution within these confines. They want to do a good job and they are looking for opportunities to exercise their skills and experience growth. As I say – especially when unemployment is at relatively low levels – people join an organisation because they want to become engaged with what they do.

But, today, this quest for engagement is done with greater and faster access to information than has ever before been the case. Employees at all levels know that, with very few exceptions, there are no 'right' or 'wrong' ways of doing things – only different ways. And they also know (or can easily discover) whether or not improvement is possible in the way their employing organisation is doing something. Accordingly Gen Y is reluctant to accept a situation in which their voices are not heard and/or in which they feel that they are not receiving the respect they believe they deserve.

1G Leaders and 2G Leaders cannot handle this. They see this as an affront – why should they respect their 'subordinates' or 'reports'? Their worldview is still enmeshed in a power and authority net – and they are the ones with the power and authority. 1G Leaders and 2G Leaders ultimately stress the importance of either 'command and control' ('do what I say') or 'responsibility and experience' ('I used to do this and I know this is how it's done. Ultimately, I'm responsible for this and if it goes wrong I don't intend to get a kick in the pants'). Under such circumstances it is not long before 'team members' become disengaged not only with their manager and fellow team members, but also with the job itself and either lower quality, reduced output and/or increased staff turnover becomes increasingly probable.

In reality teaming as we see it today is scarcely 'team work' as the theorists have advocated. Most 'teams' today are simply the traditional hierarchy functioning under different terminology. When, to this traditional hierarchy by another name, is added a situation in which team members are effectively pitted against each other so that there is internal competition (such as often happens in remuneration of sales 'teams', call centres and the like) then any real concept of cooperation and shared responsibility is even further jeopardised. In other words, the current Second Generation Leadership performance appraisal and remunerations systems (structure and human process) largely legislate against effective team operation.

In the transformation that occurred at New-way Corporation, teams became effective – one of the only two experiences I have ever had of seeing fully effective teams operating in a commercial environment. At New-way, there were still deadlines and production targets – both quantitative and qualitative. There was still a remuneration framework that rewarded different people with different organisational responsibilities in a structured way for their work. There was still a form of performance appraisal – although quite different from what had previously existed. But, in addition, now there was a free flow of information – people at all levels of New-way understood what had to be achieved, why it had to be achieved, and they had input into how it was to be achieved. People were listened to and when Ian or any other leader sought input it was with absolute authenticity. Very quickly trust developed up, down and across all organisational levels and departments. The language moved from 'us' versus 'them' to 'we' and this language shift was reflected in behaviour across the board.

Business operations conducted under a Third Generation Leadership framework have the potential to be the most innovative, creative, exciting and profitable organisations possible – teams can operate as they are supposed to. And, as New-way showed, this transformation can occur in a very short time providing the organisation's leadership is committed to the change.

But there is a second benefit to this Third Generation Leadership approach. This is the development of true professionalism.

When I ask people to define 'a professional' the responses range from 'someone whose job requires a university degree' through to 'a person who gets paid for their work'. In other words there appears to be no consensus on who is a professional and who is not a professional. I suggest that the true mark of 'a professional' is that assessment of their work is based not only on what they achieve but also on the relationship they have with their clients and fellow workers. In other words, a medical practitioner is assessed not only by whether or his or her patient recovers from an illness or injury but primarily on how the doctor relates to that patient. Similarly a lawyer is assessed not only on whether or not he or she is successful in any litigation but primarily on how the lawyer relates to that client. On the other side, of course, a person working in some manual task as well as in many functions such as research and product development is assessed primarily on whether or not that which they do has met desired results or standards.

Third Generation Leadership allows leaders (or managers if you prefer) to become true professionals. In other words, the leader is able to be assessed not only by the results achieved by the team or organisation of which he or she is the leader but also by the relationships that the leader has developed with the members of that team or organisation. If the relationship is one of openness and trust – an environment that is conducive to any high performing team and organisation – then the leader is a professional *whether or not the desired results are actually achieved.*

To fully implement this transformation in any place of work, it will help if we operate in a Third Generation Leadership world.

16

A Third Generation Leadership World

For several years of the 1970s I lived in the small New Zealand town of Feilding. Located in the Manawatu region of New Zealand's North Island, Feilding had a population of about 10,000 people and the officer in charge of the local police station was Senior Sergeant Stewart Belcher. I got to know Stewart quite well mainly through playing golf. Such social interactions led to Stewart expressing concerns about people who had problems but lacked support. At Stewart's prompting and in association with him and several others, I then became instrumental in setting up a social support centre for people with problems of any sort. Both Stewart and the rest of us were supported in this action by Feilding's then mayor, G.H. Corrick. At that time there was no formal social support of this nature available locally so this support centre was designed to be inclusive – it was independent of any group that may consciously or unconsciously seek to provide any form of political or religious influence to those they helped. We established it with the intention that it was run by the local community in premises supplied by the local council.

Stewart Belcher was one of the most pleasant people I have ever known. He also seemed to be totally non-discriminatory in his approach (as he said, he'd lock up anyone who broke the law!) and, so far as I could see, he showed unconditional respect to everyone – even those who he had to arrest (although, obviously, I have no way of knowing the complete picture).

On one occasion Stewart was recounting something that had happened. A young woman had complained of being raped and the person accused of the offence was facing court. The defence argued that because the complainant had allowed consensual sex with other men, she had no right to refuse to have sex with the accused. The defence was trying to make the case that the complainant should have complied with the defendant's wishes – that she didn't have the right to say 'yes' to some men and 'no' to another. It was being suggested strongly that Stewart should not have arrested the accused. This was put to Stewart by the defence lawyer. Stewart's response was clear. Every person, no matter their colour, creed, occupation or any other factor, should receive respect. Any woman at all, regardless of whether or not she may be a prostitute, has the right to say 'no' to sex and that 'no' must be respected. In retrospect it was a case of a lawyer with a First Generation Leadership worldview confronted by a police officer with at least a partial Third Generation Leadership worldview.

In the nineteenth century, George Rawson[1] wrote about opening one's mind to the possibility that all truth has not yet been revealed or discovered. He upset many of those in the more conservative and fundamentalist branches of Christianity by claiming that there was more truth to yet be discovered.

Although Rawson made this affirmation as part of a hymn in a Christian context (he was active in both the Congregational and Baptist Churches in England) the message of the importance of openness to change is valid across humanity in general. Whether or not we believe in a divinity, there is still much new knowledge to be had and, as humans, part of our responsibility is to seek it out and apply it.

Unfortunately there are always strong pressures from those with vested interests to restrict what we learn and what we do. Rawson, in proclaiming 'the Lord has yet more light and truth to break forth from his word' was calling for everyone in the Christian faith to be open to new understandings and new interpretations of the traditions that they were safeguarding. He was suggesting that new insights were challenging the traditional ecclesiastic structures and traditional biblical interpretations. He was crying out for everyone to be open to these new insights – to be open to change. As I say, whether or not we believe in any form of a divinity, we would do well to heed his call today – both in the religious arena and across every area of society at large.

Today all areas of virtually every nation and society are 'joined at the hip' to a worldview in which hierarchy with its accompanying power and authority emphasis is paramount. Today's world is one in which new knowledge and understanding is often rejected by many. This is especially so if it is deemed to challenge their view of the status quo of power and authority (we haven't really changed all that much since the times of Galileo!). In Graves' terms we are locked into a Level 1.3 (power), Level 1.4 (legalistic or observe the rules), Level

---

1   George Rawson (1807–89) was a solicitor in Leeds, UK.

1.5 (excel) with some elements of Level 1.6 (care for others) world. In Jaques' terms we are locked into a political, business, social and national domination by people with relatively short time spans of capacity. These people have an obvious inability to deal appropriately with the levels of complexity now being encountered. In my terms, we are locked into a Second Generation Leadership world. Red zone locus of brain control is scared of the consequences of any change and so seeks what turns out to be short term expediency even though the rhetoric may be long term.

And we wonder why we have problems!

In today's world we have political leaders from one country interfering in the affairs of other sovereign nations – often, but not always, with the best of intentions. To do this our political leaders will engineer or invent excuses and sell such excuses to their people by a mixture of partial truths and lies until they have totally obscured the real motives behind their actions – and then, no matter how disastrous the results of their interventions, they will claim that their good intentions justified the crime anyway. In this world we have some religious leaders calling for punitive action against those who propound a different view from their own and they will justify this by reference to their interpretation of what is written in their Holy Book – and expect everyone else to accept the validity of such an argument. We have other religious leaders who have sought to cover up crimes committed by their clergy and others on the grounds that allowing prosecutions would damage the authority and prestige of their faith. And we have yet other religious leaders who, based on their interpretations of their Holy Book, advocate and seek to practice serious discrimination on gender, sexual orientation and other grounds. In this world we have business leaders sometimes making money through dubious financial arrangements that ensure they will make gains even though other people suffer loss of their livelihoods, homes and self-respect – perhaps even of their lives. In this world we have other business leaders who seek to impose their wishes on governments and society regardless of what is best for their community, their nation or the world at large. In this world, on a personal level, we have an increasing incidence of debilitating illnesses such as clinical depression. In this world we have rising levels of frustration and anger in those who feel themselves powerless to get heard by the authorities in any socially acceptable way. In this world we have increasingly frequent outbursts of random acts of violence against people and property – terrorism – as those who feel themselves oppressed in some way desperately, but in totally unacceptable ways, seek to make their voices heard and to rid themselves of whatever it is that they consider to be the oppressor.

Today's world is in a mess.

Daily we witness totally unacceptable behaviour across the board and, daily, we find that unacceptable behaviour by one group is used to justify the equally unacceptable behaviour by another group. We are right. They are wrong. This is the ethos that appears to drive much of national and international policy and practice, much of religious activity, much of business activity, and much of societal behaviour.

It is now patently clear that there is no way by which these problems are able to be resolved from within our existing dominant framework. We need to approach these problems from the perspective of a new worldview; a new time span of capacity; a new generation of leadership. We need Third Generation Leadership – Leadership 3.0.

Third Generation Leadership is not a panacea. I believe there will never be a panacea nor an ultimate solution to all the problems we face. Third Generation Leadership is not the 'ultimate' leadership approach. However, Third Generation Leadership does provide us with a framework for addressing problems in a new way.

Third Generation Leadership enables us to take a new approach through shifting our brain's locus of control from the red zone to the blue zone. Third Generation Leadership moves us from a focus on 'me' or 'us' (in the very narrowest of terms) to a focus on the bigger picture – to a focus on 'us' that is genuinely inclusive. Third Generation Leadership moves us from a society that is based on power and authority to a society that is based on conceptual ability and the provision of a genuine 'value-added' component by leaders. Third Generation Leadership provides everyone with the opportunity for growth and development through transparent dealings and open communication. Third Generation Leadership respects people *as people* no matter who they are, where they are, what they believe, their sexual orientation, their colour, their religious faith (or lack of it), etc. – Third Generation Leadership is totally non-discriminatory.

If Third Generation Leadership has all these characteristics, the question arises as to why, from the 'elite' – our academics, journalists, and the like – there is no concerted pressure for change so that Third Generation Leadership becomes the norm – after all, they, too, know that existing approaches aren't working. The answer lies in the difference between 'urgent' and 'important'.

There are so many problems around – and always have been – that it is far easier (i.e. it requires far less brain energy) to operate out of the low energy usage red zone than it is to operate out of the blue zone (and by staying in the red zone of activity we can argue that 'we are doing something'). Consequently we get seduced into doing the 'urgent' rather than the 'important'.

Is it 'urgent' to deal with the threat of terrorism, or to deal with the aftermath of wars and other disasters? It certainly is. But the problem is that, far too frequently, the way in which we currently deal with such issues creates new problems – as said earlier, many of today's problems have arisen because of yesterday's solutions. I think it was Albert Einstein who said that to solve new problems we need to move out of our existing way of looking at things. And we are so busy doing what is 'urgent' that we have little or no time to do what is 'important' – like actually resolve the issues in a positive manner. Resolving issues in a positive manner and in a way that does not, of itself, cause new problems, is precisely what Third Generation Leadership is all about.

It is patently clear that many of the issues we face today have become intractable problems as we try to resolve them using our existing worldviews and leadership approaches. From a macro perspective, in 1914–1918 we had the 'war to end all wars' but 21 years later in 1939 we were at it again – the same parties in basically the same alliances, trying to resolve similar issues through violence – and failing miserably.

To illustrate this failure, consider some history over my lifetime. When I was born, the Second World War was in progress. In 1945 we had the start of the Cold War and the ongoing festering sore of the Korean conflict. We have had wars and/or civil unrest (often induced because of vested power interests) in Malaya (now Malaysia), Indonesia, Thailand, Myanmar (Burma), Cambodia, Vietnam (for 30 years!), Iraq (at least twice), Afghanistan (several times with different players and for over 20 years), Iran, Greece, Spain, Italy, The Malvinas (Falkland Islands), Sri Lanka, India–Pakistan (several times), and of course the constant irritation and intransigence of Israel and her neighbours, as well as conflicts throughout Africa and South America, and in what was once the USSR. Well may it be said 'when will they ever learn?'.[2] We have also had the rise of global terrorism which, with the paranoia that inevitably follows an inability to combat a largely unseen enemy, has, in recent days, led to serious curtailment of individual freedoms, to abuses of civil rights in developed countries, and to many in the West virtually demonising Islam and the followers of this faith.

---

2   'Where Have All the Flowers Gone?' 1961, words and music by Pete Seeger.

And, having been born during the Second World War, I have lived through every one of these examples of failure that I've listed!

But what about from a micro perspective? Over the same period, since 1939, we have had significant breakdowns in our overall social structures. In almost every country our prisons are overflowing – usually with a disproportionate number of indigenous or migrant people or of those with lower social and mental skills. We have had (and continue to have) very significant numbers of terrified people seeking to escape violence, war and persecution by becoming refugees – and we have the associated pernicious 'people trafficking' trade as some seek to make money from the misery of others. We have vast expenditure on arms with the United States spending multiples of any other country (or even of groups of other major countries combined) on weaponry – including weapons of mass destruction. The world is not how it could be whether this is considered from a personal, micro or macro perspective. I know it has always been thus.

To my readers who have very fixed religious views, I know that the Bible and other Holy Books say that wars and unrest will occur and for those of you with eschatological perspectives, I know that you see this as a sign of the end of the times and, for some, of the Parousia. I know that therefore you are not particularly perturbed by such international strife. Rather you tend to embrace it because you see it as one of the indicators of the Parousia. You see wars and turmoil (particularly in the Middle East) as leading towards something for which you yearn. But a religious faith is not only about eschatology and what eventually happens to 'me'. Surely, at least as much as about some form of 'pie in the sky when you die', a religious faith should about improving the quality of life – here and now – for everyone today as well as for tomorrow!

To my ultra conservative readers, I know that you have strong feelings about what is 'right' and what is 'wrong'. I know, too, that you feel threatened because acknowledging that, despite your best efforts, things still aren't working the way you would like is a challenge to the way in which you want to do business and to the way you want the world to be. I understand your retreat to First and Second Generation Leadership worldviews and I understand how you want to preserve what you hold dear and important. But there really is more to life than power, money and the status quo.

To my politician readers, I know that most of you enter politics for the very best of reasons – you genuinely want to make positive change and to ensure good government. But doing what is best for everyone (with 'everyone' used in a very broad sense of the word) is far more complex than joining a political party and engaging in party politics. In the long run, the very essence of party politics degenerates to the issues around being re-elected to govern or, in the worst-case scenario, minimising the time out of power. But doing what is best for the people is not necessarily consistent with policies and practices espoused and practised by any one political party or coalition of parties – or indeed even of what occurs primarily only within national borders.

We don't need any form of world government imposed by some dominant country or political/social/religious power. No country has the right to dictate to another country how it should act – especially when dual standards are used by the country making the demands. Despite apparent beliefs to the contrary, no country or political/social/religious power actually has the role of 'world's policeman' in which they (and their allies), operating from a prejudiced 'we are right perspective' can determine what behaviour in or by another country is acceptable or unacceptable and almost demonise those with whom they disagree. The worldviews that underpin any concept of 'world policeman', 'empire' or domination are those of power and hierarchy – they are First Generation Leadership models implemented by Second Generation Leaders. As is obvious from the response to many world conflict situations, attempts to be the world's policeman are increasingly rejected both by those who are seeking their own First Generation Leadership or Second Generation Leadership approach to domination as well as by those of us seeking a Third Generation Leadership world. But in a world dominated by Third Generation Leadership thinking and behaviour bodies such as the United Nations could operate as they were intended to operate – free from dominance by any one country or group of countries and where, by dialogue and honest dealing most, if not all, international issues could be resolved without bullying or other use of force. In other words, the United Nations could function as it was intended to function when it was established and the power of veto by a few powerful nations in the Security Council would no longer be used primarily to push that country's own political or international agenda but rather for the overall good of everyone.

When will we be mature enough to say 'enough is enough'? The system is broken and needs mending – and it's well past the stage where 'band-aids' will suffice to persuade the gullible that, deep down, everything is really ok.

It's time we started to focus on what is important right now as well as in the future – not just on some vision or hope that may questionably be grounded in today's reality. It's time that, together, we started to focus on how, in every way, we can make this a better world not only for us, but, far more importantly, for our grandchildren's grandchildren. And for this to happen we need a huge shift in the way we think and act.

A better world will not be devoid of problems. A Third Generation Leadership world is not some form of 'Shangri-La' or 'utopia' – I do not believe that such a perfect world ever has existed nor ever will exist. A Third Generation Leadership world will still have problems because people are people and all people have differing worldviews depending on what they are facing or have encountered and on the overall situation in which they find themselves. But a Third Generation Leadership world will be a world in which we seek new solutions to the problems that emerge. A Third Generation Leadership world will utilise the knowledge from neuroscience and have the blue zone as its default position. A Third Generation Leadership world will be a world that embraces new thinking. A Third Generation Leadership world will be a world in which respect and engagement can flourish. A Third Generation Leadership world will be a world of new behaviours that pays serious attention to the long-term impacts of today's decisions. A Third Generation Leadership world will be one which seeks to deal with ambiguity and complexity in a positive way not only for the present situation but also for the benefit of those generations that are yet to come.

It's time for a Third Generation Leadership world – for 3G Leadership – for Leadership 3.0.

17

Facilitating the Shift to a Third Generation Leadership World

In May 2010 there was a massive crude oil leak disaster on an oil rig leased by the oil giant, BP, in the Gulf of Mexico. The Deepwater Horizon rig operated and owned by contractor Transocean exploded and sank, killing 11 men and triggering the leak. In the hours after the accident, BP and the US Coast Guard said there appeared to be no leak, but their estimate of the amount of oil being discharged into the ocean was later revised to first 1,000, then 5,000, barrels per day. In June 2010, US government scientists raised estimates for the amount coming from this leak to 40,000 barrels per day (by some estimates roughly 6.5 million litres per day) from the earlier revised forecast of 20,000 barrels. The US Coast Guard then accused BP of failing to have the right equipment and back-up plans and Rear Admiral James Watson of the US Coast Guard blamed BP for lacking the necessary equipment to capture all the oil flowing from its catastrophic leak.

The negative effect of this disaster on the physical environment was immense. Plumes of oil formed beneath the surface of the ocean and the oil slick drifted in the wind and currents to affect shorelines, flora and wildlife as well as threatening the US state of Florida and other countries such as Cuba. Those in some US areas bordering the Gulf of Mexico and relying on the sea for their livelihoods had their sources of income at least temporarily removed and entire communities faced the possibility of total devastation. There was also, to use a term so loved by the military, 'collateral damage' in that the value of BP stock plunged and its shareholders had their dividends affected because BP will be paying for the cleanup as well as compensation to all those who have lost their livelihoods – and those costs will probably be in the tens of billions of dollars.

Of course, this was not the first time offshore oil rigs have had problems. Over the years there have been issues from time to time in the North Sea and as recently as 2009 there was a serious problem close to Australia when the West

Atlas oil rig in the Timor Sea, operated by the Thai-owned PTTEP Australasia, blew on 21 August and leaked over 400,000 litres of oil, gas and condensate into the Timor Sea at a rate reported variously as being from 300 to 1,200 barrels a day.

Unfortunately oil spill disasters are not new. On 24 March 1989, the Exxon Valdez, an oil tanker en route to Long Beach California hit a reef in Alaska's Prince William Sound and spilled an estimated minimum 40.9 million litres (or 250,000 barrels) of crude oil. Until recently, this was considered to be one of the most devastating human-caused environmental disasters ever to occur. The oil eventually covered 2,100 km of coastline and 28,000 km^2 of ocean.

Given that both the history of and the potential for disaster was well known and clearly documented, why was BP's response in the Gulf of Mexico so poor? The leak was capped and stopped in July 2010 and while at the time of writing full investigation into the spill is on-going and all the facts are not known, it does seem reasonable to assume that inadequate attention had been paid to any 'worst-case' scenarios. I suggest that this is totally in accord with the Second Generation Leadership worldview that dominates both big business and the political scene. In Gravesian terms (Chapter 7) a Level 3 (power) and Level 5 (excel) view dominates and, in Jaques' terms (Chapter 10) those in charge do not operate at the conceptual thinking stratum level necessary for dealing with the degree of ambiguity and complexity that is involved.

Events like this are tragic and they should further focus our attention on the necessity to shift our leadership understanding and approach.

Third Generation Leadership is fully cognisant of the need to run organisations profitably. There is no conflict between economic success and Third Generation Leadership.

The difference in Third Generation Leadership approaches from those of First Generation Leadership and/or Second Generation Leadership lies in the path to this success. Third Generation Leadership sees the overall interaction between all the systems at play – both in the short term and the very long term – and then seeks, in practice as well as in theory, to ensure that any negative implications are minimised both now and in the future.

A Third Generation Leadership in an oil drilling operation would seek to have detailed and appropriate contingency plans ready for immediate implementation in the event of accidents occurring. In this scenario, everyone close to any point of possible disaster would have the requisite knowledge and authority to take action to avert possible disaster in the event of warning signs becoming apparent – and alarms would not be disabled. At the same time these people would have the authority to immediately implement the contingency plans in the event of a disaster erupting. BP certainly had such plans but something appears to have been missing. Given that in this Gulf of Mexico disaster there appears to be evidence that, only days before the disaster, some engineers on the Deepwater Horizon rig had warned about faulty valves, it seems that something was lacking. If the authority to immediately implement remedial or some additional preventative action had existed at BP and had been available on the Deepwater Horizon rig in May 2010 perhaps the devastation that occurred could have been totally averted. At the very worst, the environmental and economic damage may have been significantly reduced.

The time is ripe for facilitating a shift to a Third Generation Leadership worldview as our dominant paradigm.

The process for this facilitation is really quite simple:

- What are the things that we believe need changing in today's world?

- What are the behaviours that caused the current situation?

- What behaviours can we change?

- What ought these new behaviours to be?

- How can we learn these new behaviours?

- What is each of us individually going to do in order to bring about these new behaviours?

- What are the implications of this for our own personal behaviour as a leader?

First, what are the things that we believe need changing in today's world? In today's litany of world problems, where does one start? Let's see, religious fundamentalism/extremism and/or fanaticism and intolerance (no matter whether the faith involved is Christian, Jewish, Muslim, Hindu, Buddhist, or any other), the Israeli–Palestinian situation, the invasion of Iraq and its consequences of death and maiming for so many Iraqis and non-Iraqis, Afghanistan, Iran, North Korea, nationalism, prejudice, refugees, 'scientific' whaling research, indigenous people's rights, poverty, exploitation, terrorism – the list goes on and on and every person will have their own ideas as to what are problems that can and should be resolved and what are those problems that are in the 'too hard basket' and so should be ignored or to which only lip service should be applied. As I have said before, the evidence is clear – our existing approach is broken and needs fixing.

Second, what are the behaviours that caused the current situation? There are still those today (both individuals and countries) who seem to operate on a 'born to rule' type approach. These are the people and nations who demand obedience to their demands or compliance with their wishes. This is totally a First Generation Leadership or a Second Generation Leadership mindset. It is all about control and getting what 'I' want (at least in the short term) and in which longer term implications, while discussed, are generally dismissed or given only cursory attention because 'I' am mainly concerned about maximising profits or maintaining my power now and in the immediate future. These are the people who persist in doing what has been done before even when it manifestly fails to achieve desired results. They are seen in the 'law and order' debate in which the emphasis is on punishing offenders rather than looking at new, possibly innovative, crime prevention strategies that are designed to keep as many people as possible from offending through the provision of education, jobs, and the development of their sense of self-worth. They are seen in the 'them' and 'us' dichotomy in which 'we' are right and 'they' are wrong. They are seen in arguments where 'we' are good but 'they' are bad. They are seen in politics where you are labelled either 'right wing' or 'left wing'. They are seen in arguments where everyone falls into one of two camps – either 'for' me or 'against' me (where 'me' can equally be an individual, a faith, a country, or an organisation). Because in this worldview only 'us' matter and those in power reserve the right to define 'us' in as broad or as narrow a way as we wish depending on the extent to which such definition helps us attain our goals. Think about the few examples I have already given (religious fundamentalism, extremism and/or fanaticism and intolerance (no matter whether the faith involved is Christian, Jewish, Muslim, Hindu, Buddhist, or any other), the Israeli–Palestinian situation, the invasion of Iraq and its consequences of death and maiming for so many Iraqis and non-Iraqis, Afghanistan, Iran, North Korea, nationalism, prejudice, refugees, 'scientific' whaling research, indigenous people's rights, poverty, exploitation, terrorism) and ponder on how many of these are directly caused by such behaviours – usually by all parties involved.

Third, what behaviours can we change? The good news about behaviours is that they can all be changed. Can you teach an old dog new tricks? You sure can. The issue is one of creating a situation in which the old dog wants to learn new tricks and then working patiently to teach them and to enable the dog to show them off.

Rugby Football League (RFL) is a very tough, rough, physically and mentally demanding game with 13 players in each team (none of whom wear any significant form of protective gear other than mouthguards) played primarily in Australia, New Zealand, Papua New Guinea, France and Great Britain. In Australia, other than national representation, the pinnacle is to be selected to play for your state in the annual State of Origin series – three matches played in various locations with players usually selected on the basis of the state in which they were born or where they played their first games rather than on their state of residency.

In the week ending 13 June 2010 the RFL world was shattered when one of the New South Wales (NSW) players, Timana Tahu, withdrew from the NSW team – 'the blues' – only days before they were due to play Queensland ('the reds') in the second of the 2010 series. Rumours were rife with 'personal reasons' being cited as the reason for the withdrawal. Then the weekend papers of 12 and 13 June released the full story. It transpired that at a practice session during the week, one of the NSW assistant coaches – a man who, as a player, was once a giant of the game – made a comment which Tahu felt racially slurred both a member of the Queensland team and another man who had recently decided to change the type of football he played (he moved from RFL to Australian Rules Football in late 2011). Tahu, a close friend of one of the people who was slurred, was deeply upset both because of the racial slur (he had been aware of them before but this was the last straw) and because of the attack on his friend. After taking a few days to consider the best action, he decided that only his withdrawal from the team would suffice to demonstrate the depth of his repugnance and concern. Tahu was rightly being hailed by most people as a hero who was prepared to make a considerable personal sacrifice in standing up for what is right. The assistant coach resigned and there were serious questions as to whether or not he would ever again be involved in any way with the game.

Now not even his most ardent supporters would argue that Timana Tahu is a saint or indeed is a 'blue zone person', but it seems to me that, at least in this instance, Tahu took a very 'blue zone' approach to this behavioural problem of racism. He made his objection to the comment clear at the time but then took time to reflect on what was the best way of dealing with the situation. He found a different way from that which anyone would have expected and, rather than instituting legal proceedings of any sort, ensured by his actions that the matter received the maximum attention required and that the matter was resolved. Tahu's action should guarantee that the final vestiges of racism and prejudice that may still exist in this game will now receive the attention that is required and that ever more stringent efforts will be made to change the behaviours of those who act inappropriately both in regard to racial issues as well as to those who exhibit any other form of prejudice.

Tahu created a situation in which new behaviours could be learned and could come to the fore.

The key behaviours that we need to learn in order to operate in a Third Generation Leadership manner are those which enable us to focus our brains' areas of control in the blue zone rather than the red zone. Such a shift will enhance our ability to find innovative and new solutions to present and emerging problems.

Fourth, what ought these new behaviours to be? I have said before that getting rid of what you don't want is quite different from getting what you do want. A blue zone approach, however, is not prescriptive in terms of specific behaviours. Rather it is descriptive in terms of setting out the broad picture and allowing each person to determine for him or herself the behaviours that best fit. And in terms of 'descriptive behaviours', the behaviours that we need are those that demonstrate an awareness of the total system in which we all live.

We live in an interacting social system that can be illustrated by the well known 'chaos theory' in which, in general terms, it is argued that the overall impact of a butterfly flapping its wings in Africa can cause a storm thousands of kilometres away in the Americas. We need leadership that, while being very aware of local concerns and issues and ensuring appropriate attention is paid to these, is also aware of the broader impact. Such leadership seeks to minimise the potential negative impact on other people and places. We need, too, leadership which considers the long-term implications of whatever is done today. We need leadership that has the requisite level of thinking to deal with the increasingly complex world in which we live. In every arena of life, we need leadership that can deal with ambiguity and complexity in a way that is ultimately beneficial for everyone and everything – not just our immediate cronies or those to whom we owe political allegiance and/or power.

Fifth, how can we learn these new behaviours?

In Chapter 9 I suggested that the way forward was to learn new communication skills. I suggested that Third Generation Leaders learn the skills of:

- powerful questioning;

- observational listening;

- optimistic listening.

This is because:

- powerful questioning shows respect for the other person;

- observational listening shows people that they are being listened to;

- optimistic listening shows belief in the other person.

And these three attributes[1] are those which create an environment in which both we and those with whom we interact are able to grow. They are the core skills of Third Generation Leadership.

The sixth and seventh questions:

- What is each of us individually going to do in order to bring about these new behaviours?

- What are the implications of this for our own personal behaviour as a leader?

I must leave to my readers to answer for themselves.

---

1   Full information as to how these skills can be developed is found in Mowat et al., *The Success Zone*.

Epilogue

John Lennon wrote the song 'Imagine' – an idealistic vision of what things could be. 'Imagine' has been criticised or endorsed depending on the philosophical bent of the listener with some arguing that such an approach would herald a form of worldwide communism and others arguing for it being a dream that could inspire mankind to change the way in which we interact with each other.

There is a sense in which I have some things in common with John Lennon. I can see that what we have is not working. I see a widening gap between rich and poor: between east and west; between 'haves' and 'have nots'; between those with power and those without power. I see extensive exploitation of people and the world's resources. And I don't like it. Fortunately I'm not alone.

John Lennon nominated a world with equality. Possible very nice in theory but I can't see it as being either realistic or attainable. And John Lennon failed to provide any form of suggestion as to how his idealistic world could come about.

I think it was Thoreau who said something like: 'Build your castles in the air: that is the place for them. But then put the foundations under them'. That is what I have tried to do.

Third Generation Leadership is a foundation for building a better world – one that we can be proud to leave to our grandchildren and our grandchildren's grandchildren. It won't happen overnight, but, with enough people committed to bring about the change we need, it can happen.

But, as I have said, if we are going to bring about Third Generation Leadership we need to consider a few questions:

- What are the things that we believe need changing in today's world?

- What are the behaviours that caused the current situation?

- What behaviours can we change?

- What ought these new behaviours to be?

- How can we learn these new behaviours?

- What is each of us individually going to do in order to bring about these new behaviours?

- What are the implications of this for our own personal behaviour as a leader?

I've already made some suggestions in relation to most of these questions. Now I must leave the individual answers to these questions to you.

You can help bring about a Third Generation Leadership world – a Leadership 3.0 world – by becoming a Third Generation Leader. As US president, Barack Obama, said in the days leading up to his 2008 election:

Can we do it? Yes we can!

Appendices

Additional Resources

Some additional background reading that may be of interest is:

Barnett, Thomas P.M. *Great Powers: America and the World After Bush*, Putnam, USA, 2009.

Beck, D. and Cowan, C. *Spiral Dynamics. Mastering Values, Leadership and Change*, Blackwell Publishers Inc., USA, 1996.

Bennis, Warren, ed. *Leaders on Leadership: Interviews with Top Executives*, Harvard Business Review, USA, 1992.

Cope, Mick. *The Seven Cs of Coaching*, Pearson Education Ltd, USA, 2004.

Corrigan, John. *A World Fit For Children*, Castleflag Pty Ltd, Sydney, 2005.

Dixon, Norman. *On The Psychology Of Military Incompetence*, Random House, London, 1976.

Doidge, Norman. *The Brain that Changes Itself*, Scribe Publications, USA, 2010.

Frankl, Victor. *Man's Search for Meaning*, Hodder & Stoughton Ltd, USA, 1964.

Gadiesh, Orit and MacArthur, Hugh. *Lessons from Private Equity Any Company Can Use*, Bain & Company, Inc. Harvard Business Press, USA, 2008.

George, Bill (with Peter Sims). *True North: Discover Your Authentic Leadership*, Jossey-Bass, San Francisco, 2007.

Harvey-Jones, Sir John. *The Company Chairman*, Director Books, UK, 1995.

Jaques, Elliott. *Requisite Organisation*, Cason Hall & Co, USA, 1998.

Jaques, Elliott. *Time Span Handbook*, Heinneman, London, 1964.

Jaques, Elliott and Clement, Stephen D. *Executive Leadership: A Practical Guide to Managing*, Basil Blackwell, Inc., Cambridge, MA, 1991.

Kandel, Eric. *Principles of Neural Science*, 4th edn, McGraw-Hill, USA, 2000.

Lehrer, Jonah. *The Decisive Moment*, Canongate Books Ltd, Edinburgh, 2009.

Long, D.G. *Leaders: Diamonds or Cubic Zirconia?* Centre for Leadership Studies, Sydney, 1998.

Long, D.G. *Learner Managed Learning: The Key to Lifelong Learning and Development*, Kogan Page, London and St Martins Press, New York, 1990.

Lynch, D. and Kordis, Paul L. *Strategy of the Dolphin*, Ballantine Books, USA, 1990.

McGregor, Douglas. *The Human Side of Enterprise*, McGraw-Hill, Kogakusha Ltd., Tokyo, 1960.

Miller, Alice. *For Your Own Good*, Farrar, Straus and Giroux, New York, 1990.

Mowat, Andrew, Corrigan, John and Long, Douglas. *The Success Zone*, Global Publishing, Melbourne, 2010.

Moyes, Allan. *Quality Leadership*, The Centre for Leadership Australia, Sydney, 1997.

Rock, David. *Quiet Leadership*, Collins Publishers, USA, 2006.

Rogers, Carl. *On Becoming A Person*, Houghton Mifflin Company, USA, 1961.

Schwartz, Barry, Wasserman, Edward A. and Robbins, Steven J. *Psychology of Learning and Behaviour*, 5th edn, W.W. Norton & Co., USA, 2001.

Scott, Susan. *Fierce Conversations: Achieving Success at Work*, Viking Penguin, New York, 2002.

Wexler, B.E. *Brain and Culture: Neurobiology, Ideology, and Social Change*, MIT Press, Cambridge, MA, 2006.

The Research Underlying the Book

The concepts presented in this book were developed from a research programme led by one of my colleagues, John Corrigan of Group 8 Education – a wholly owned business of Group 8 Management Pty Ltd – a company in which I both have a financial interest and am a director.

In the early 2000s, Corrigan decided to dedicate 10 years to transforming education. He made this decision after participating in a Sydney Leadership Program conducted by The Benevolent Society of NSW where he had become concerned about the issue of the earnings and status of teachers.

A study of the available literature indicated that virtually all studies conducted in Australia and overseas sought to ascertain parent, student and community views of teachers and teaching from the base of believing that 'the system' was fine and that the problems, if any, were caused by teachers, parents and a decline in community values. Pressure groups of teachers, parents and others then sought to validate their own position with the result that conflict focused on peripheral or, in Deming's terms, 'special' causes or issues such as remuneration, school conditions, funding and curriculum rather than confront the system's problems.

A loop had developed which resulted in a downward spiral of confidence in teachers and the state education system and allowed bodies with vested interests (such as the non-government school system) to flourish even though, in fact, the education provided by non-government schools was not appreciably better (in real terms) than that of government schools.

Corrigan decided to challenge this. An approach was needed that had no a priori assumptions as to the causes of the problem and which would seek to discover causes and solutions whether they were 'systems' issues or 'special' issues – ideally it should combine qualitative and quantitative approaches.

The decision was made to:

- investigate a real situation in a school that acknowledged there were problems in student behaviour, school attendance and academic results to get an indication of what the real issues might be;

- get hard data as to perceptions of 'good' teachers and schools;

- using an action research approach, validate these opinions within the broadest possible base of schools and parents;

- based on this data, develop an approach for remedying the situation and trial this with schools across every socio-economic strata.

In 2004 a market research company was commissioned to conduct an Australia-wide random survey of parents, teachers and students asking each person surveyed to describe their ideal school and their ideal teacher. The data from this were then subject to factor analysis and from this three questionnaires were developed – one each for parents, teachers and students.

The questionnaires were then used in an action research project to develop organisational capability. This action research programme involved trialling ways of bringing about the shift in behaviour that was necessary if the ideal school sought by teachers, parents and students was to be attained. In the early stages the emphasis was on individual change but, as the project progressed, it became apparent that both individual teachers and school culture needed attention and change. This then focused attention on leadership – the hub around which revolved everything impacting on performance.

Over the period 2005–2007 this programme was then initially administered to 50 schools (almost all Secondary Schools) in Victoria – government and Catholic including four Koori (Aboriginal) schools and encompassing every socio-economic grouping in the state:

- approximately 80 teachers per school;

- approximately four parents per teacher per school;

- 20 students per gender per year (approximately 240 students per school).

The survey was administered in such a way that qualitative data provided the issues and prioritised these while quantitative data provided how well schools performed in relation to each of these factors. It became obvious that, to thrive, a student needs to be engaged in their own learning. It was also clear that when a student is engaged in their own learning the following behaviours are observable in that student:

- confidence in themselves;

- respect for their teacher; and

- a desire to go out of their way not to disappoint or let down their teacher.

It is freedom from fear combined with specific attitudes, behaviours and skills of teachers that engage students in their own learning.

This work was then taken to the United Kingdom in a project known as The High Performing School Programme where almost identical results were obtained. This led to some schools promoting their experience through descriptive case studies. In December 2008, Woodham Community Technical College in the UK reported:

> *The implementation of the High Performing Schools programme at Woodham Community Technology College was as part of a pilot programme endorsed by the local authority.*

The programme started in the spring term 2007.

Senior staff at the school firmly believed that the programme would improve the school culture and ethos and help to raise standards across the school. They understood the commitment involved and that the improvements would be seen over a period of time.

The information gathered for this case study has highlighted a number of areas of improvement which are listed below:

- *Improved staff collaboration and professional dialogue.*
- *A positive change in areas of professional development for staff, such as personal confidence, management techniques, engagement with pupils, perceptions of 'learning' and 'education', classroom practice and job satisfaction.*
- *Improved ethos both for adults and students in the school.*
- *Improved student attitudes and behaviour in the classroom.*
- *Student perception of 'feeling safe' had risen.*
- *An improvement in persistent absenteeism data, now lowest in the area.*
- *FFT data shows significant improvement in some areas.*
- *RAISEonline data shows significant positive change in various areas including: CVA Key Stage 3-4, Percentage of candidates achieving 5 or more A*–G at GCSE and equivalent, Attainment, Average capped (Best 8) Points Score at Key Stage 4 Special Educational Needs.*

The school's involvement with Group 8 Education and the High Performing Schools Programme has changed the culture and outlook of the school. Issues where, in the past, there was little understanding of a process for change, have become foci for change.

The elements of Staff and Student Voice, alongside student feedback have provided a vehicle for whole school understanding and collaboration.

Cognitive Coaching has encouraged professional dialogue and closer working relationships, alongside nurturing the attitudes and behaviours necessary to foster a culture of respect.

The school fully understands that the process has not ended and they now have the skills and understanding to sustain the programme year on year. The nature of the programme allows a fully supportive online resource provided through Group 8 Education.

The overall aim of the case study is to produce a report on how one school has experienced the High Performing School's Programme and to see what, if any change, has taken place as a result.

The context statement has been written by the school and details the rationale behind the adoption of the programme as well as the school's experience in implementing it.

The data used for the case study was collected through interviews with senior staff who were involved in implementing the programme, middle leaders who were involved in coaching and leading on the development groups, junior staff who, although not directly involved with the organisation of the programme, did experience some elements and a variety of students. Alongside this a number of school data sources were analysed.

The first part of the analysis is of statements and questionnaires submitted by the aforementioned groups. The second part deals with the analysis of school data sets and the conclusions we may draw as to outcomes of the programme.

In October 2011, Woodham released a further case study showing progress since 2007:

Woodham Community Technology College

Context

Woodham Community Technology College is a secondary school in Newton Aycliffe, County Durham. There are around 800 students on roll, almost all white British. Attainment on entry is broadly average, 21% of students are eligible for free school meals and 26% have special educational needs.

In January 2006, Ofsted judged the school to be 'satisfactory'. There was a clear need to improve. In September 2007, Woodham began working with Group 8 Education. The aim was to change the culture of the school to create the conditions for sustained improvement. As a result of the 'High Performing Schools programme', now known as The Success Zone™ programme, the school:

- *Established a clear vision understood by all.*
- *Aligned values across the school community.*

- *Established a distinctive culture based on unconditional mutual respect.*
- *Began a programme of teacher development based on cognitive coaching.*

Four years on, the impact of the programme is measurable:

- *Year on year improvement in results.*
- *5 A* - C 80% + 26% from 2007, 5 A* - C including English & Maths, 52%, + 11% from 2007.*
- *All groups of students make progress at least in line with expectations.*
- *The gap between FSM and other students is closing rapidly.*
- *Year on year improvement in attendance which is now high.*
- *Steady decline in persistent absenteeism – 6.2% in 2007, 2.4% in 2011.*
- *54% drop in fixed term exclusions over last 2 years.*
- *Reported behaviour incidents declined by 55% over the last 2 years.*
- *Proportion of observed lessons judged as outstanding 18% in 2009/10, 32% in 2010/11.*

An Ofsted inspection in September 2011, judged that Woodham Community Technology College is a good school that is improving strongly. The following quotes from the report highlight the success of Group 8 Education's input:

- *Students, staff, parents and carers are most positive about the school.*
- *The quality of teaching has also improved and is good. There is some outstanding practice in teaching and learning within the school.*
- *Students are welcoming and proud of their school.*
- *One student told inspectors, 'The teaching has improved, so you really want to come to school now'.*
- *Learning and progress are good overall and sometimes outstanding. Expectations are high and students enjoy a challenge. Their behaviour contributes well to their learning.*
- *Students are in no doubt that they feel safe in school.*
- *When asked to describe their school, one student replied, 'the people here make this school what it is – friendly relationships, but teachers are strict when necessary'.*
- *The school is rightly proud of its good care, guidance and support and its reputation as an inclusive school.*
- *Very strong leadership team with high expectations where roles and responsibilities are clearly understood and skilfully woven together.*
- *Staff morale is high. Comments such as, 'the atmosphere in the school is fantastic' and 'this school is on a relentless upward trajectory' indicate the satisfaction and level of commitment of the staff. It is therefore, no surprise that that the school has made great strides towards its goals.*

•   *Parents and carers are overwhelmingly positive about the school and value greatly the openness and approachability of the staff.*

In a 2009 case study, Iramoo Primary School, in Victoria, Australia – a school in one of the more socio-economically disadvantaged areas of Melbourne – reported that as a direct result of their involvement in this programme, their school results had made the following shift according to a State Department of Education survey (see Figure A.1).

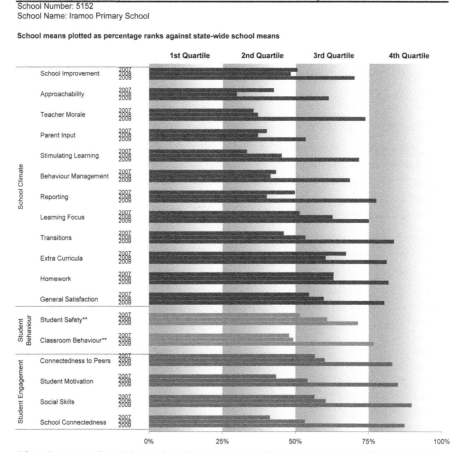

Figure A.1   Victorian State Department of Education, Iramoo Primary School results

Iramoo quoted teachers as saying:

> *Iramoo Primary School staff is well on the journey to establishing a 'blue zone' environment thanks to The Success Zone and Andrew's working relationship/coaching over the past few years. As we identify and understand our own emotions and those of others we are developing the skills to have effective conversations for successful outcomes. We are building a deeper awareness of triggers affecting the zones and skills to listen & communicate to focus on operating in the 'blue zone' (Raquel Tweedley and Nella Cascone, Iramoo Primary School).*

> *By all staff and students understanding two key aspects of the brain, teachers and leaders are able to activate the areas responsible for engagement and high achievement, while knowing what areas of the brain to avoid (Moira Findley, Principal).*

John Corrigan, Andrew Mowat and I wondered whether the knowledge gained from the education arena had a wider application. The concepts were discussed and the process trialled in Australia with organisations in both the for-profit and not-for-profit sectors. The data from these confirmed that the issues relating to engagement and improving overall performance were basically the same in the commercial arena as they were in the education field. This led to the development of what I call Third Generation Leadership.

Index

For Product Safety Concerns and Information please contact our EU representative GPSR@taylorandfrancis.com Taylor & Francis Verlag GmbH, Kaufingerstraße 24, 80331 München, Germany

Printed and bound by CPI Group (UK) Ltd, Croydon, CR0 4YY

08/05/2025

01864522-0004